PHONICS
Grade 1

Table of Contents

PHONICS

Grade 1

Mary Lou Maples, Ed.D.
Chairman of Department of Education
Huntingdon College
Montgomery, Alabama

Credits:
McGraw-Hill Children's Publishing Editorial/Production Team
Vincent F. Douglas, B.S. and M. Ed.
Tracey E. Dils
Jennifer Blashkiw Pawley
Teresa A. Domnauer
Tracy R. Paulus
Suzanne M. Diehm

Big Tuna Trading Company Art/Editorial/Production Team
Mercer Mayer
John R. Sansevere
Erica Farber
Brian MacMullen
Matthew Rossetti
Billy Steers
Diane Dubreuil
Atomic Age, Inc.

McGraw-Hill
Children's Publishing
A Division of The McGraw-Hill Companies

Send all inquiries to: McGraw-Hill Children's Publishing, 8787 Orion Place, Columbus OH 43240-4027

1-57768-821-X

3 4 5 6 7 8 9 10 GRAY 05 04 03 02 01

WELCOME TO CRITTERVILLE!

Spider

Frog

Grasshopper

Mouse

Little Critter

Little Sister

Dad

Kitty

Mom

Dog

Gator

Bat Child

Gabby

Bun Bun

Tiger

Maurice

Molly

Malcolm

Review: S, M, and T

Name __Becky__

Name the pictures. Write the letter that stands for the beginning sound of each picture name.

m   s   t

s   t   m

m   t   s

Skill: Review of sound-symbol association of initial **s**, **m**, and **t**

Ending Sounds: S, M, and T

Name _____

The sound at the end of **bus** is spelled by the letter **s**.

The sound at the end of **ham** is spelled by the letter **m**.

The sound at the end of **cat** is spelled by the letter **t**.

| bus |
| ham |
| cat |

Look at the pictures. Circle the letter that stands for the sound you hear at the end of the picture name.

s m (t)	s (m) t	s m (t)	(s) m t
s (m) t	s (m) t	(s) m t	s m (t)
s m (t)	(s) m t	s (m) t	(s) m t
s m (t)	s (m) t	(s) m t	s m (t)

Skill: Sound-symbol association of final **s**, **m**, and **t**

Review: P, N, and C

Name

Name the pictures. Write the letter that stands for the beginning sound of each picture name.

n

c

p

c

n

p

p

p

n

Skill: Review of sound-symbol association of initial **p**, **n**, and **c**

Ending Sounds: P, N, and C

Name_____

The sound at the end of **moon** is spelled by the letter **n**.

The sound at the end of **mop** is spelled by the letter **p**.

The sound at the end of **magic** is spelled by the letter **c**.

| moon |
| mop |
| magic |

Name the pictures. Circle the letter that stands for the sound you hear at the end of each picture name.

p (n) c	p (n) c	p n (c)	(p) n c
(p) n c	p n (c)	(p) n c	(p) n c
p (n) c	(p) n c	p (n) c	p (n) c
(p) n c	p (n) c	(p) n c	(p) (n) c

Name_____

Name the pictures. Write the letter that stands for the beginning sound of each picture name.

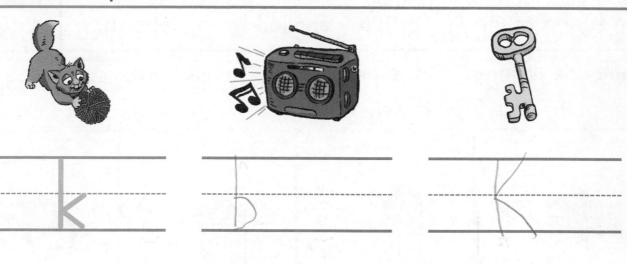

k

b

K

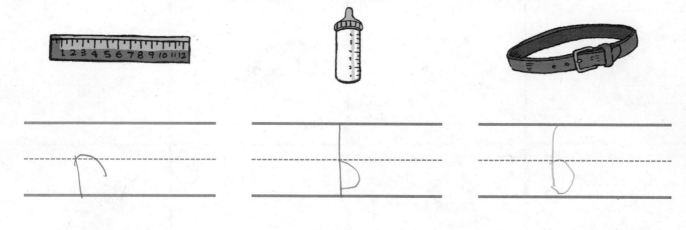

r

b

b

r

r

K

Skill: Review of sound-symbol association of initial k, r, and b

Ending Sounds: K, R, and B

Name_____

The sound at the end of **book** is spelled by the letter **k**.

The sound at the end of **four** is spelled by the letter **r**.

The sound at the end of **tub** is spelled by the letter **b**.

book
four
tu**b**

Name the pictures. Circle the letter that stands for the sound you hear at the end of each picture name.

	k r (b)		k (r) b		k (r) b		k (r) b
	k (r) b		k r (b)		k (r) b		k r (b)
	(k) r b		k r (b)		k r (b)		(k) r b
	k (r) b		k (r) b		(k) r b		k (r) b

10

Skill: Sound-symbol association of final **k**, **r**, and **b**

Review: J, F, and G

Name_____

Name the pictures. Write the letter that stands for the beginning sound of each picture name.

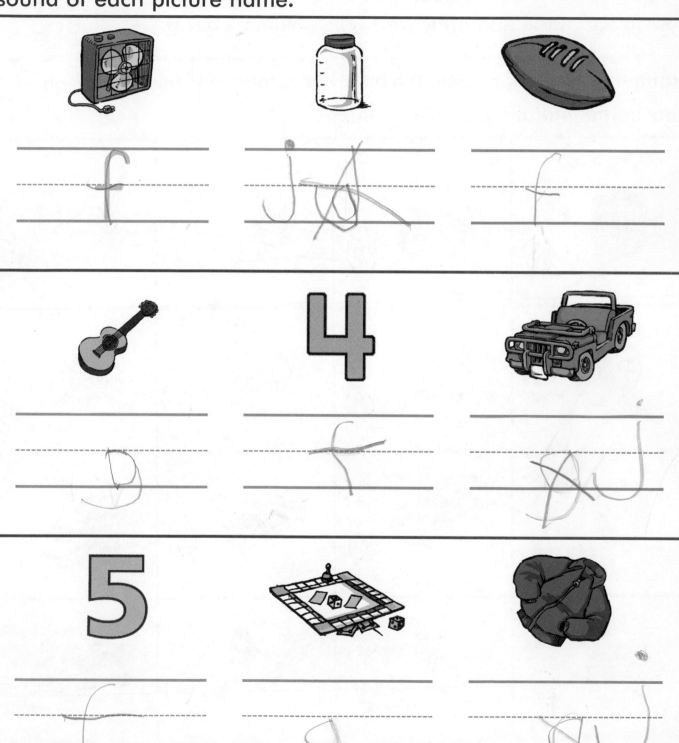

f

j

f

D

f

J

f

g

J

Skill: Review of sound-symbol association of initial **j**, **f**, and **g**

Ending Sounds: F and G

Name_____

The sound at the end of **roof** is spelled by the letter **f**.
The sound at the end of **bag** is spelled by the letter **g**.

| roof |
| bag |

Name the pictures. Circle the letter that stands for the sound you hear at the end of each picture name.

f	f (g)	(f) g	f (g)
(f) g	f (g)	(f) (g)	f (g)
f (g)	f (g)	f (g)	(f) g
f (g)	(f) g	f (g)	f (g)

Skill: Sound-symbol association of final **f** and **g**

Review: H, D, and Z

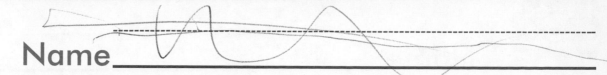

Name_____

Name the pictures. Write the letter that stands for the beginning
sound of each picture name.

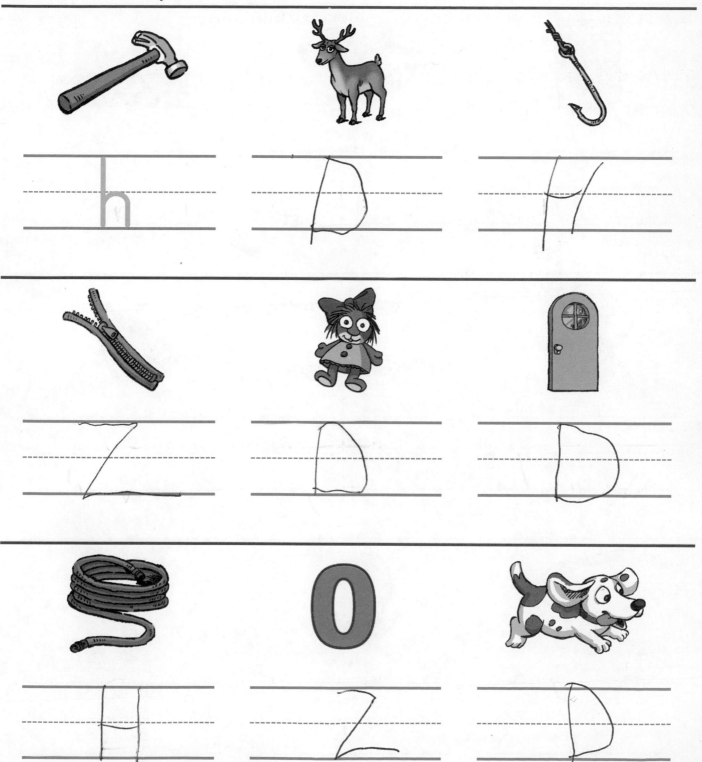

Skill: Review of sound-symbol association of initial **h**, **d**, and **z**

Review: V, W, and L

Name_____

Name the pictures. Write the letter that stands for the beginning sound of each picture name.

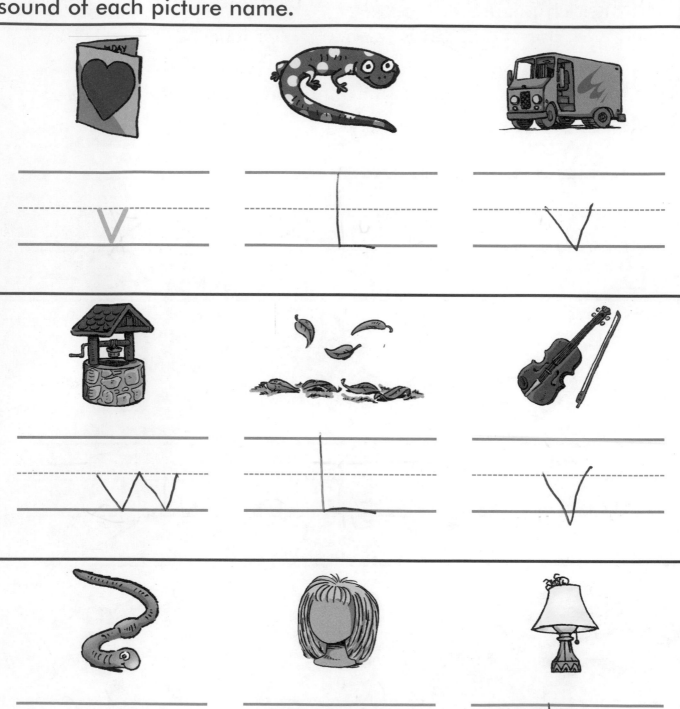

Skill: Review of sound-symbol association of initial v, w, and l

Ending Sounds: D and L

Name_____

The sound at the end of **road** is spelled by the letter **d**.

The sound at the end of **girl** is spelled by the letter **l**.

road
girl

Name the pictures. Circle the letter that stands for the sound you hear at the end of each picture name.

d ⓛ	ⓓ l	ⓓ l	d ⓛ
ⓓ l	d ⓛ	d ⓛ	ⓓ l
d ⓛ	ⓓ l	d ⓛ	ⓓ l
d ⓛ	d ⓛ	d ⓛ	ⓓ l

Skill: Sound-symbol association of final **d** and **l**

Review: Y and Qu

Name_____

Look at the pictures. Write the letter or pair of letters that stands for the beginning sound of each picture name.

qu   qu   Y

?   Y   Y

Y   Y   qu

Skill: Review of sound-symbol association of initial **y** and **qu**

Review: Ending Sounds

Name_____

Name the pictures. Write the letter that stands for the ending sound of each picture name.

m   d   n

g   l   b

p   r   s

Skill: Review of sound-symbol association of final consonants

Progress Check: Consonants

Name_____

Name the pictures. Write the letters that stand for the beginning and ending sounds of each picture name.

dog   nut   mop

fox   bat   sun

ham   lid   rug

Skill: Assessment of sound-symbol association of initial and final consonants

Short A

Name_____

Fan has the short-a sound. This sound is usually spelled by the letter a.

fan

Name the pictures. Circle each picture whose name has the short-a sound.

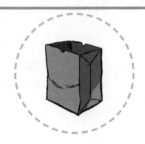  

Skill: Auditory discrimination of short a

Short A

Name_____

Name the pictures. Write **a** below each picture whose name has the short-**a** sound.

fan

_____

a

_____

a

_____

_____

a

_____

_____

a

_____

a

_____

a

_____

Skill: Sound-symbol association of short **a**

Short A

Name_____

Read the words and name the pictures. Draw a
line from each word to the picture it names.

f**an**

bag
bat

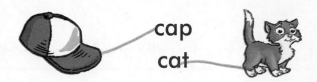
cap
cat

hat
ham

map
mat

tag
ax

van
man

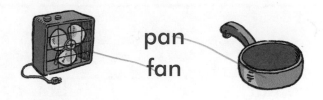
pan
fan

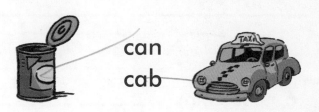
can
cab

Skill: Symbol-sound association of short-**a** words

Short A

Name _____

Read each sentence and the words beside it.
Write the word that makes sense in each sentence.

f**an**

1. The van is __tan__ .

tan
man
ran

2. Bat Child likes the blue __hat__ .

sat
mad
hat

3. I sat on the big __mat__ .

mat
at
am

4. The __man__ is Gabby's dad.

bat
man
fan

5. Grandma has a red __fan__ .

am
fan
has

6. Malcolm __sat__ in the back.

ham
sat
bat

Skill: Short-a words in context

Short I

Name_____

Bib has the short-**i** sound. This sound is usually spelled by the letter **i**.

bib

Name the pictures. Circle each picture whose name has the short-**i** sound.

         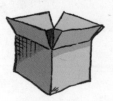

Skill: Auditory discrimination of short i

Short I

Name the pictures. Write **i** below each picture
whose name has the short-**i** sound.

bib

i

24

Short I

Name

Read the words and look at the pictures. Draw a line from each word to the picture it tells about.

bib

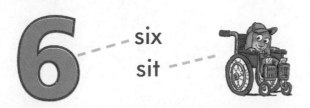

six
sit

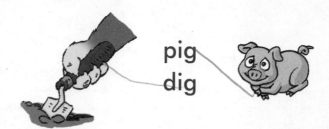

pig
dig

mitt
mix

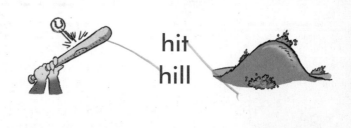

hit
hill

wig
win

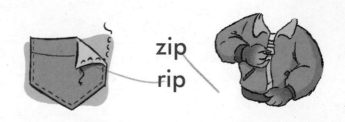

zip
rip

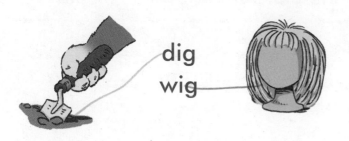

dig
wig

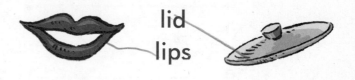

lid
lips

Skill: Symbol-sound association of short-i words

Short I

Name _____

Read each sentence and the words beside it.
Write the word that makes sense in each sentence.

bib

1. Will this hat _____fit_____ Little Critter?

fit
wig
did

2. Mr. Critter will _____fill_____ the car with gas.

wig
his
fill

3. Little Critter said his cat was _____it_____ .

ill
is
if

4. The pig _____hid_____ on the hill.

six
kid
hid

5. Little Sister _____hit_____ the ball with the bat.

hit
his
pin

6. Is the _____lid_____ on the pan?

hills
lid
him

Skill: Short-i words in context

Review: Short A and I

Name_____

Read the words and look at the pictures. Circle the word that tells about each picture.

pin fan fin (pan)	hit mat mitt (hat)	(lid) lad lap lip
sit (ax) add six	bat bit miss mad	hit bag hat big
cat tap (cap) tip	pig dad dig pass	wag dig (wig) dad
mix fat (map) fit	rip sap sip ran	(can) zip cap big

Skill: Review of symbol-sound association of short-a and short-i words

Short O

Name _____

Top has the short-o sound. This sound is usually spelled by the letter o.

top

Name the pictures. Circle each picture whose name has the short-o sound.

Skill: Auditory discrimination of short o

Short O

Name_____

Name the pictures. Write **o** below each picture whose name has the short-**o** sound.

top

_____

O

_____

O

_____

_____

10

_____

_____

O

_____

O

_____

O

_____

Skill: Sound-symbol association of short **o**

Short O

Name _____

Read the words and look at the pictures. Draw a line from each word to the picture it tells about.

top

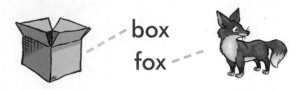

box
fox

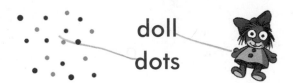

doll
dots

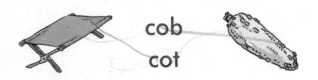

cob
cot

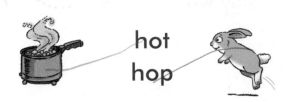

hot
hop

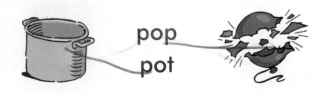

pop
pot

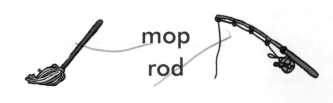

mop
rod

ox
top

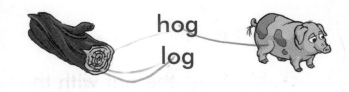

hog
log

Skill: Symbol-sound association of short-o words

Short O

Name _____

Read each sentence and the words beside it.

Write the word that makes sense in each sentence.

top

1. The doll is in the **box** .
   - box
   - odd
   - hog

2. Molly wants to help with the ___hot___ pot.
   - stop
   - hot
   - log

3. The ___fox___ sat on a log.
   - fox
   - lot
   - hot

4. Maurice will get the ___cot___ for you.
   - on
   - odd
   - cot

5. Mom got the ___mop___ for my dad.
   - not
   - mop
   - on

6. Gabby likes the hat with the blue ___dots___ .
   - dots
   - hot
   - lot

Short E

Name _____

Bed has the short-**e** sound. This sound is usually spelled by the letter **e**.

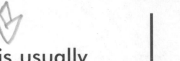

bed

Name the pictures. Circle each picture whose name has the short-**e** sound.

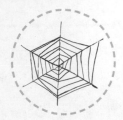   

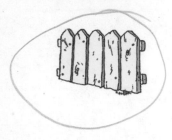    

Skill: Auditory discrimination of short **e**

Short E

Name _____

Name the pictures. Write **e** below each picture whose name has the short-**e** sound.

b**e**d

e

i

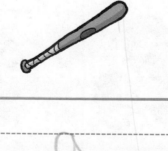

e   a   o

Short E

Name _____

Read the words and look at the pictures. Draw a line from each word to the picture it tells about.

bed

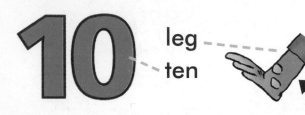

leg
ten

wet
jet

bell
well

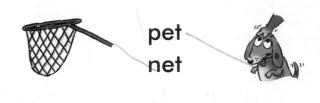

pet
net

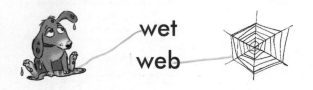

wet
web

egg
fell

men
hen

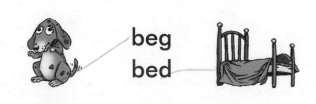

beg
bed

Short E

Name _____

Read each sentence and the words beside it.
Write the word that makes sense in each sentence.

b**e**d

1. Little Sister _**fed**_ the cat.

| jet |
| web |
| fed |

2. Is the _jet_ set to go?

| met |
| fed |
| jet |

3. Dad will let Little Critter get a _pet_ .

| pet |
| fell |
| web |

4. Is the pig in the _pen_ ?

| beg |
| pen |
| wet |

5. Tiger will help fix the _eggs_ .

| eggs |
| fell |
| let |

6. We _met_ at the play.

| met |
| get |
| let |

Skill: Short-e words in context

35

Review: Short O and E

Read the words and look at the pictures. Circle the word that tells about each picture.

(box) fed bell fox	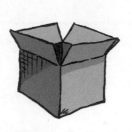	top (ten) men mop	**10**	(jet) pot job pet	
hot men hen (mop)		doll pet (well) pot		(egg) ox fell fox	
wet (web) cob cot	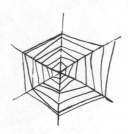	(pop) ten top pen		tell beg (top) bed	
rod leg (log) red		fed hop (hen) mop		got (net) not get	

Skill: Review of symbol-sound association of short-o and short-e words

Short U

Name _____

Cup has the short-u sound. This sound is usually spelled by the letter u.

cup

Name the pictures. Circle each picture whose name has the short-u sound.

Skill: Auditory discrimination of short u

Short U

Name _____

Name the pictures. Write **u** below each picture whose name has the short-**u** sound.

cup

u

e

u

u

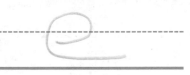

a

u

i

u

u

Skill: Sound-symbol association of short **u**

Short U

Name_____

Read the words and look at the pictures. Draw a line from each word to the picture it tells about.

cup

 bus
sun

 bun
bug

 tub
hug

 run
rug

 cup
pup

 cut
cub

 mud
mug

nut
jug

Skill: Symbol-sound association of short-u words

39

Short U

Name_____

Read each sentence and the words beside it.
Write the word that makes sense in each sentence.

cup

1. Bun Bun put the pup into the ___tub___ .

cub
tub
cut

2. The cub fell into the ___mud___ .

mud
run
nut

3. Gator put the ___cups___ and mugs into a box.

cuts
sun
cups

4. Malcolm had to ___run___ to get help.

run
tub
mug

5. Little Critter will fix the ___cut___ on his leg.

cut
jug
sun

6. Gabby got the can of ___nuts___ for Mom.

cuts
nuts
mug

Review: Short Vowels

Name_____

Read the words and name the pictures. Circle the word that names each picture.

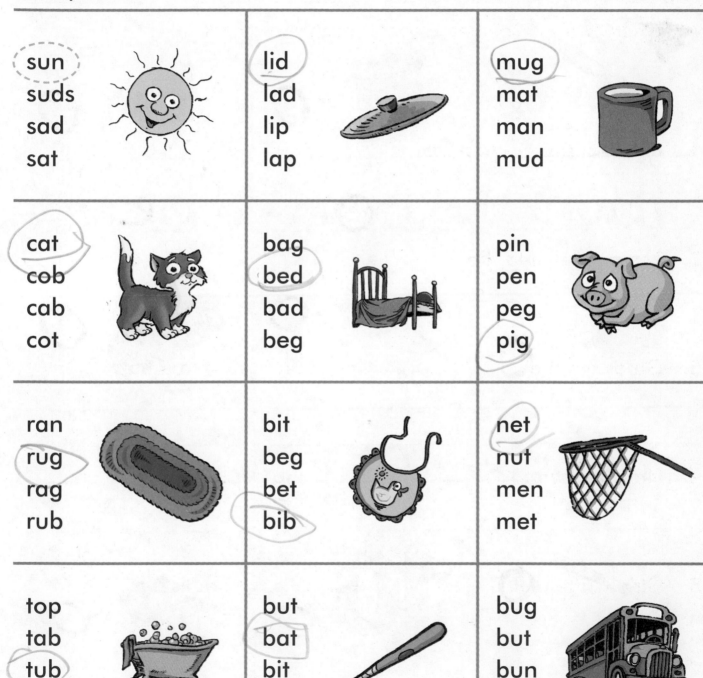

(sun) suds sad sat	lid lad lip lap	mug mat man mud
cat cob cab cot	bag bed bad beg	pin pen peg pig
ran rug rag rub	bit beg bet bib	net nut men met
top tab tub tap	but bat bit bet	bug but bun bus

Skill: Review of symbol-sound association of short-vowel words

Short Vowels

Name the pictures. Circle the letter that stands for the vowel sound in each picture name. Then write the letter to complete the picture name.

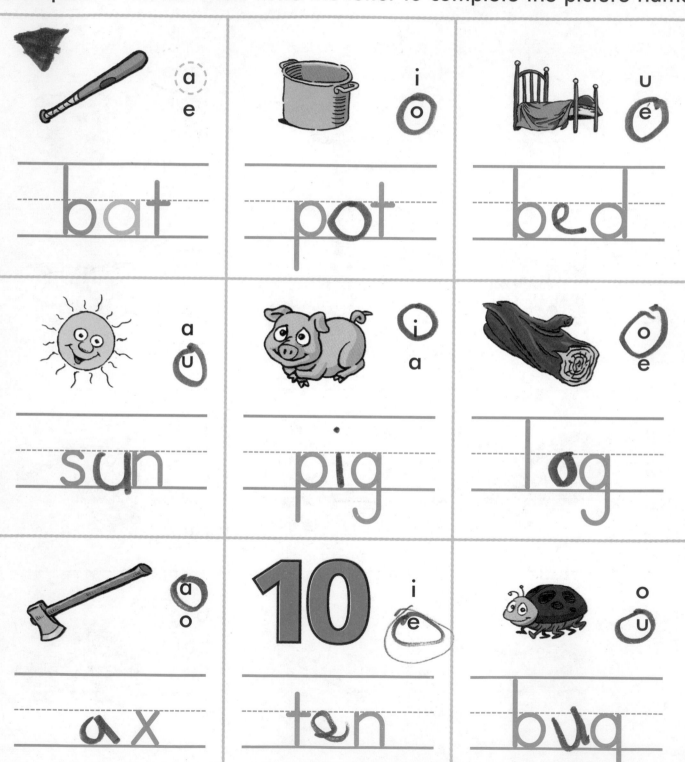

a *(e)*	i *(o)*	u *(e)*
bat	pot	bed
a *(u)*	*(i)* a	*(o)* e
sun	pig	log
(a) o	i *(e)*	o *(u)*
ax	ten	bug

42

Short Vowels

Name _____

Circle the word that names each picture. Then write the word in the blank.

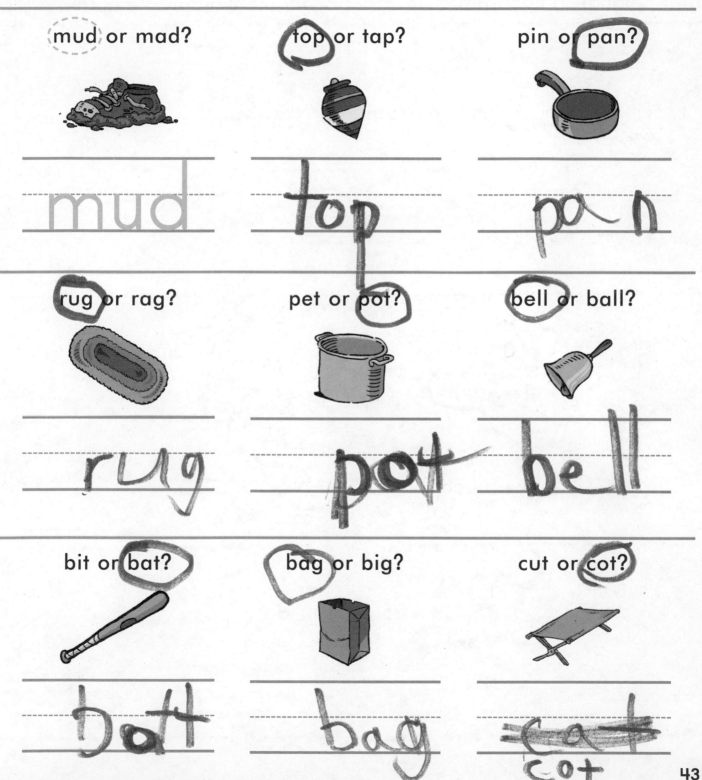

(mud) or mad?   top or tap?   pin or pan?

mud   top   pan

rug or rag?   pet or pot?   bell or ball?

rug   pot   bell

bit or bat?   bag or big?   cut or cot?

batt   bag   cot

Skill: Symbol-sound association of short-vowel words: a, e, i, o, u

Short Vowels

Name _____

Read the sentences and the words under the blanks. Circle the word that belongs in each sentence. Then write the word in the blank.

1. Little Critter wants to make the <u>**bed**</u> .
   (bed)   bad

2. The pig fell into the <u>~~mud~~</u> . *mud*
   (mud)   mad

3. The <u>doll</u> is in a big box.
   hill   (doll)

4. Mom will make a bed for the <u>cats</u> .
   (cats)   cuts

5. The <u>fox</u> ran into its den.
   (fox)   fix

6. Molly had on her tan <u>cap</u> .
   cub   (cap)

44

Short Vowels

Name _____

Read the sentences and look at the pictures. Draw a line from each sentence to the picture it tells about.

 The cat plays with the rag.
                       The cat plays with the rug.

 Dad has the mop.
                        Dad has the map.

 The dog has the bell.
                        The dog has the ball.

 Little Sister got the bug.
                       Little Sister got the bag.

 Little Critter has a red cup.
                        Little Critter has a red cap.

 Mom will fix the ham.
                       Mom will fix the hem.

Skill: Short-vowel words in context

Long A

Rake has the long-a sound. This sound is often spelled by **a** and silent **e**.

rake

Name the pictures. Circle each picture whose name has the long-a sound.

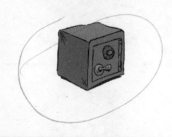   

46

Long A

Name_____

Name the pictures. Write the letter or letters to complete each picture name.

fan   rake

cave   cap   cape

lake   vase   fan

pan   bat   gate

Skill: Sound-symbol association of long **a**

Long A

Name _____

Read the words and name the pictures. Draw a line from each word to the picture it names.

fan   rake

can
cane

ape
tape

cap
cape

cave
cat

gate
game

rake
lake

vase
wave

man
mane

48

Long A

Name_____

Read each sentence and the words beside it.
Write the word that makes sense in each
sentence.

fan   rake

1. Gator _____ate_____ the ham.

| at |
| ate |
| am |

2. Is the _____bat_____ in the cave?

| make |
| bat |
| mad |

3. Mother wants to fix the _____gat_____ .

| get |
| gave |
| gate |

4. Did you play the _____game_____ ?

| game |
| gate |
| gas |

5. Gabby will fix the pen with _____tape_____ .

| tape |
| tap |
| take |

6. I have the _____pan_____ for the mix.

| pan |
| rake |
| pat |

Skill: Long-a words in context

Long I

Name _____

Kite has the long-i sound. This sound is often spelled by **i** and silent **e**.

k**ite**

Name the pictures. Circle each picture whose name has the long-i sound.

Skill: Auditory discrimination of long i

Long I

Name_____

Read the words and look at the pictures. Draw a line from each word to the picture it tells about.

bib   kite

 hive
five **5**

9 line
nine

 bike
bite

tire
fire

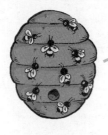 kites
pipes

 vine
pine

 ride
wire

dive
dime

51

Skill: Symbol-sound association of long-i words

Long I

Name

Name the pictures. Write the letter or letters to complete each picture name.

 bib   kite

 line    dime    pig

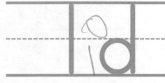 lid    hive    vine

six    bike    hill

Skill: Sound-symbol association of long i

Long I

Name _____

Read each sentence and the words beside it.
Write the word that makes sense in the
sentence.

bib   kite

1. Tiger will __dive__ into the lake.

     did
     dive
     dime

2. Do you like to play with __kites__?

     kit
     kites
     kiss

3. The __hive__ is in the pines.

     hive
     hid
     hide

4. Gabby will __fix__ the tire on the car.

     fire
     fix
     file

5. I like to hike in the __hills__.

     hive
     hills
     hid

6. Malcolm will __ride__ on his bike.

     ripe
     rid
     ride

Skill: Long-i words in context

Review: Long A and Long I

Name_____

Read the words and look at the pictures. Circle the word that tells about each picture.

time tin tap (tape)		kit can kite (cane)		dim (dime) date dam	
pan (van) vine pine		bit (bike) bite big		(ride) rat ran rid	
hide (hive) hat hate	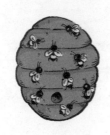	miss (mat) mitt man		(dive) dad did date	
lad lid like (lake)		sat side (safe) sit		(pine) pin pal pale	

54

Skill: Review of symbol-sound association of long-a and long-i words

Long O

Name_____

Bone has the long-o sound. This sound is often spelled by o and silent e.

bone

Name the pictures. Circle each picture whose name has the long-o sound.

Skill: Auditory discrimination of long o

Long O

Name_____

Read the words and look at the pictures. Draw a line from each word to the picture it tells about.

top   bone

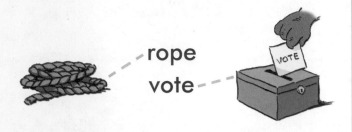
rope
vote

poke
pot

home
hop

cone
bone

note
robe

hose
hole

pole
pop

rose
nose

Skill: Symbol-sound association of long-o words

Long O

Name_____

Name the pictures. Write the letter or letters to complete each picture name.

top   bone

note   rose   fox

robe   mop   cot

top   rope   hole

Skill: Sound-symbol association of long o

57

Long O

Name _____

Read each sentence and the words beside it.
Write the word that makes sense in the
sentence.

top   bone

1. Dad put the _rose_ into the vase.

| rob |
| rose |
| nose |

2. We hope you will tell us the _joke_ .

| joke |
| hop |
| poke |

3. Molly _rode_ to the game with Maurice.

| rod |
| rope |
| rode |

4. Bun Bun put the red robe in a _box_ .

| bone |
| box |
| mop |

5. Did you _vote_ for Gator or Tiger?

| not |
| note |
| vote |

6. Bat Child _got_ the bone for his dog.

| go |
| got |
| good |

58

Skill: Long-o words in context

Long U

Name_____

Tube has the long-u sound. This sound is often spelled by **u** and silent **e**.

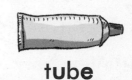

tube

Name the pictures. Circle each picture whose name has the long-**u** sound.

 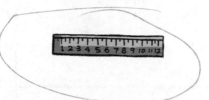 

  5

Skill: Auditory discrimination of long **u**

Long U

Name _____

Read the words and look at the pictures. Draw a line from each word to the picture it tells about.

cup   tube

 mud
mule

rug
mug

 cub
cube

run
ruler

  cut
cute

tune
bun

 tub
tube

bus
bug

Skill: Symbol-sound association of long-u words

Long U

Name _____

Look at each picture. Write the letter or letters to complete the word that tells about the picture.

cup   tube

mule   cube   cup

bug   tune   cute

tube   tub   rug

Skill: Sound-symbol association of long **u**

Long U

Name _____

Read each sentence and the words beside it.
Write the word that makes sense in each
sentence.

cup   tube

1. Tiger likes to ride on the _____mule_____ .

| mug |
| mule |
| mud |

2. Can you play this _____tune_____ ?

| tub |
| tune |
| tube |

3. I will use my dimes for the _____bus_____ ride.

| bus |
| bug |
| bun |

4. Put the _____cube_____ in the cup.

| cub |
| cute |
| cube |

5. I _____cut_____ my leg on the gate.

| cup |
| cute |
| cut |

6. What are the _____rules_____ of the game?

| rugs |
| rules |
| rubs |

Skill: Long-u words in context

Review: Long O and Long U

Read the words and name the pictures. Circle the word that names each picture.

cub cob cone (cube)	rode (ruler) rod run 	top toss tube (tub) 
(mop) mug mole mule 	note (nut) not nose 	(mule) mug moss mole 
rule (rose) rod rug 	bone but (bus) box 	(top) tune tug tone 
rule run (rope) rot 	(bone) box bus bun 	(note) nut nose not

Skill: Review of symbol-sound association of long-o and long-u words

Review: Long Vowels

Name_____

Name the pictures. Write the letters to complete each picture name.

hive   rope   tube

note   mule   cube

bone   vine   like

64

Skill: Review of sound-symbol association of long vowels

Long Vowels

Name _____

Read each sentence and the words beside it. Write the word that makes sense in the sentence.

1. Nine bats are in the __cave__ .

   cave
   came
   note

2. I may _____ a cape.

   vote
   make
   kite

3. What is his _____ ?

   name
   five
   nine

4. The lid is on the _____ .

   time
   tune
   tube

5. Did you _____ into the lake?

   dive
   hive
   live

6. The puppy wants to _____ the bone.

   line
   hope
   hide

Skill: Long-vowel words in context

Long Vowels

Name _____

Circle the word that tells about each picture. Then write the word in the blank.

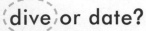 dive or date?

 dive

cube or cape?

_____

cone or cane?

_____

---

rode or rope?

_____

cute or cave?

_____

line or lake?

_____

---

rake or rope?

_____

time or tape?

_____

ride or rose?

_____

Skill: Symbol-sound association of long-vowel words

Long Vowels

Read the sentences and name the pictures. Write the word that names each picture.

1. It sounds like **line**.      It is a __nine__ .

2. It sounds like **name**.   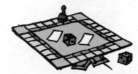   It is a _____ .

3. It sounds like **tube**.   It is a _____ .

4. It sounds like **rake**.      It is a _____ .

5. It sounds like **five**.   It is a _____ .

6. It sounds like **cone**.      It is a _____ .

Skill: Sound-symbol association of long-vowel words

Long Vowels

Name _____

Read the words below. Then name the pictures. Write the word that names each picture.

nine	tube	note
wave	rake	hive
bone	bike	cube

tube

Skill: Symbol-sound association of long-vowel words

Long Vowels

Name _____

Look at each picture. Circle the letters that stand for the vowel sound. Then write the letters to complete the word that tells about the picture.

a – e (circled) o – e	u – e i – e	a – e o – e
r a k e	d __ v __	r __ b __
a – e i – e	u – e o – e	o – e a – e
s __ f __	b __ n __	t __ p __
i – e a – e	u – e o – e	u – e a – e
b __ k __	m __ l __	g __ m __

Skill: Sound-symbol association of long vowels

Long Vowels

Read the sentences and look at the pictures. Draw a line from each sentence to the picture it tells about.

Little Critter rode the mule.
Little Critter rode the bike.

The rose is in the vase.
The vine is in the vase.

The dog has a bone.
The dog has a kite.

Gator plays a tune.
Gator plays a game.

The rope is on the bed.
The tube is on the bed.

Little Sister has on a cape.
Little Sister has on a robe.

Skill: Long-vowel words in context

Long Vowels

Name _____

Name the pictures. Write the letters to complete each picture name.

t u b e   c _ p   b _ n

r _ s   m _ l   _ _ n

c _ n   b _ k    h _ v

Skill: Sound-symbol association of long vowels

71

Long Vowels

Name _____

Read the words and name the pictures. Circle the word that names each picture.

(rope) rake rule ripe	bone bake bite bike	rose rise rake rope
date dime dive dine	cube cone cove cane	tape tube take tale
take tube tore time	wire wore vane vine	tube tune tame tale
name nine nose note	rude ride rode ruler	nose note name nine

72

Short and Long Vowels

Name_____

Name the pictures. Write the letter or letters to complete each picture name.

vine   r   s   l   k

   **5**

w   b   f   v   f   x

      **10**

m   l   b   b   t   n

Skill: Sound-symbol association of short and long vowels

Short and Long Vowels

Name_____

Read the words and name the pictures. Draw lines from the words to the pictures they name.

 pan pale pad		nose not note	
cat cave came		rose robe rob	
 bike bib bite		cube cut cub	
man mane map		pine pig pin	

Skill: Symbol-sound association of short- and long-vowel words

Short and Long Vowels

Name _____

Read each sentence and the words beside it. Write the word that makes sense in each sentence.

1. Did you ride the __bike__ ?

    bit
    bite
    bike

2. Put on the red _____ .

    rob
    rug
    robe

3. Tell Little Critter to _____ the kite.

    fix
    fox
    five

4. I have _____ dimes to save.

    net
    nine
    name

5. The _____ ran into the den.

    fat
    fox
    fine

6. Put the _____ on the pot.

    lid
    like
    line

Skill: Short- and long-vowel words in context

Short and Long Vowels

Name _____

Read the sentences and name the pictures. Write the word that names each picture.

1. It sounds like **bite.**      It is a  _kite_ .

2. It sounds like **fan.**      It is a _____.

3. It sounds like **cot.**   It is a _____.

4. It sounds like **red.**      It is a _____.

5. It sounds like **nose.**   It is a _____.

6. It sounds like **save.**      It is a _____.

Skill: Sound-symbol association of short- and long-vowel words

Short and Long Vowels

Name

Read the words below. Then name the pictures. Write the word that names each picture.

nine	rose	bat
pig	hive	cube
box	cane	sun

sun

Skill: Symbol-sound association of short- and long-vowel words

77

Short and Long Vowels

Name

Read the sentences and look at the pictures. Draw a line from each sentence to the picture it tells about.

The cap is on the bed.
The cape is on the bed.

Put the can in the box.
Put the cane in the box.

The cat bats at the tub.
The cat bats at the tube.

Little Sister has the kit.
Little Sister has the kite.

Little Critter sees the cub.
Little Critter sees the cube.

Let me take the tag.
Let me take the tape.

78

Progress Check: Short and Long Vowels

Name_____

Name each picture. Write the letter or letters to complete the word that names the picture.

cave

l___k

p___g

j___t

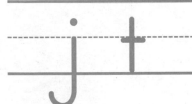

r___p

n___n

t___b

s___n

f___n

Skill: Assessment of sound-symbol association of short and long vowels

S Blends

Name_____

In some words, the letter **s** comes before another consonant. To say these words, blend the sound of **s** with the sound of the consonant that follows it.

stop   skate
smile   **sleep**

Look at the pictures. In each row, circle the picture or pictures that begin with the same sound as the first picture.

Skill: Auditory discrimination of initial **s** blends: **st, sm, sk, sl**

S Blends

Name

Read the words below. Then look at the pictures. Write the word that tells about each picture.

sled	skip	step	smoke	stem
skate	stone	slide	smile	

stem

Skill: Symbol-sound association of initial s-blend words: st, sm, sk, sl

S Blends

Name_____

In some words, the letter **s** comes before another consonant. To say these words, blend the sound of **s** with the sound of the consonant that follows it.

scare snap
swim spin

Look at the pictures. In each row, circle the picture or pictures that begin with the same sound as the first picture.

Skill: Auditory discrimination of initial s blends: sc, sw, sn, sp

S Blends

Name_____

Read the words below. Then look at the pictures. Write the word that tells about each picture.

spill   snake   scale   snip   spell

snap   scare   swim   spin

scare _____ _____

_____ _____ _____

_____ _____ _____

Skill: Symbol-sound association of initial **s**-blend words: **sc, sw, sn, sp**

Review: S Blends

Read the words and look at the pictures. Circle the word that tells about each picture.

slim (skip) snip swim 	smell swell spell still 	spine smile skid slide 
spoke stone smoke slope 	swim slim spin skin 	stop slap skip snap 
spill swell smell still 	snake state scale spare 	spin skin slim swim 

Skill: Review of symbol-sound association of s-blend words: **st, sm, sk, sl, sc, sw, sn, sp**

L Blends

Name_____

In some words, the letter l follows another consonant. To say these words, blend the sound of the first consonant with the sound of l.

flower
play

Name the pictures. In each row, circle the picture or pictures that begin with the same sound as the first picture.

Skill: Auditory discrimination of initial l blends: **fl, pl**

L Blends

Name _____

Read the words below. Then look at the pictures. Write the word that tells about each picture.

play	plate	flag	flute	plane
plug	flame	flat	plum	

ƒlute _____ _____

_____ _____ _____

_____

_____ _____ _____

Skill: Symbol-sound association of initial l-blend words: **fl, pl**

L Blends

In some words, the letter l follows another consonant. To say these words, blend the sound of the first consonant with the sound of l.

clown
blue
glad

Look at the pictures. In each row, circle the picture or pictures that begin with the same sound as the first picture.

Skill: Auditory discrimination of initial l blends: **cl, bl, gl**

L Blends

Name_____

Read the words below. Then look at the pictures. Write the word that tells about each picture.

clip	blade	globe	clam	glass
club	clap	class	glad	

club

88

Review: L Blends

Name_____

Read the words and name the pictures. Circle the word that names each picture.

(clip) flap glad plan 	clap blaze glass flame	flute plate blade glad
glare plane flame blade 	plane flake blame clam 	play clap flag glad 
club plug flag glad 	flake plate blame glare 	globe blob club plug 

Skill: Review of symbol-sound association of initial l-blend words: fl, pl, cl, bl, gl

R Blends

Name_____

In some words, the letter **r** follows another consonant. To say these words, blend the sound of the first consonant with the sound of **r**.

frog
brown
green

Name the pictures. In each row, circle the pictures that begin with the same sound as the first picture.

90

R Blends

Name _____

Read the words below. Then look at the pictures. Write the word that tells about each picture.

grab	frog	bride	grade	grape
grill	grin	frame	graze	

bride _____   _____

_____   _____   _____

_____   _____   _____

Skill: Symbol-sound association of initial r-blend words: **fr, br, gr**

R Blends

Name_____

In some words, the letter **r** follows another consonant. To say these words, blend the sound of the first consonant with the sound of **r**.

cry   pretty
dress tree

Look at the pictures. In each row, circle the picture or pictures that begin with the same sound as the first picture.

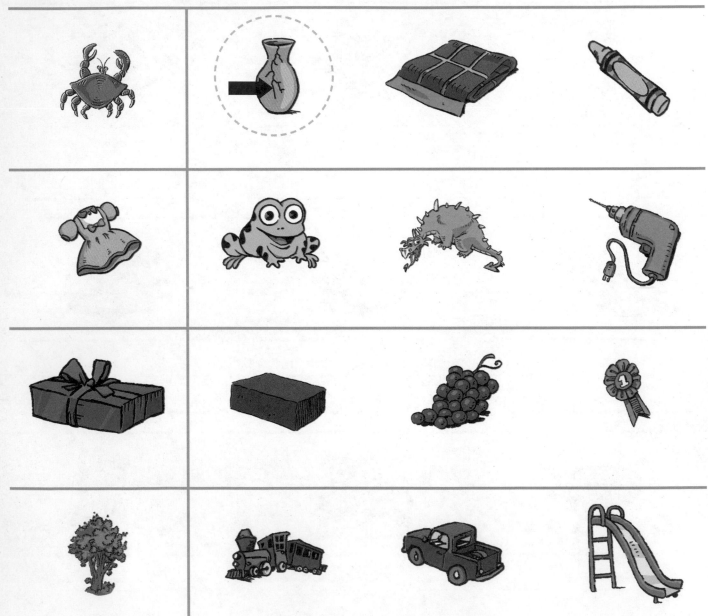

92

R Blends

Name_____

Read the words below. Then look at the pictures. Write the word that tells about each picture.

trip   trap   crib   drip   crab

dress   drill   drum   prize

drip

Skill: Symbol-sound association of initial r-blend words: **cr, dr, pr, tr**

Review: R Blends

Name_____

Read the words and look at the pictures. Circle the word that tells about each picture.

(grapes)
brave
trade
frames

from
drum
grab
crate

grill
drip
crib
trap

---

crab
grass
trap
drag

prize
bride
drive
trade

drag
frog
crop
grab

---

prize
bride
froze
drive

grin
trim
drum
from

graze
prize
prune
bride

Skill: Review of symbol-sound association of initial r-blend words: fr, br, gr, cr, dr, pr, tr

Final S Blends

At the end of some words, the letter **s** comes before another consonant. To say these words, blend the sound of **s** with the sound of that consonant.

ask
just

Look at the pictures. In each row, circle the picture or pictures that end with the same sound as the first picture.

Skill: Auditory discrimination of final s blends: st, sk

95

Final S Blends

Name_____

Read the words below. Then look at the pictures. Write the word that tells about each picture.

list	nest	fist
mask	cast	desk
crust	vest	tusk

vest

_____

_____

_____

_____

_____

EGGS
MILK
BREAD

_____

_____

_____

Skill: Symbol-sound association of final s-blend words: st, sk

Review: Final S Blends

Name_____

Read the words and look at the pictures. Circle the word that tells about each picture.

test nest task (tusk) 	cast crust dust desk 	list last test tusk
cost cast mask most 	pest nest must mask	most desk dust mask
tusk test vest most 	desk ask mask must 	fast task fist tusk 

Skill: Review of symbol-sound association of final s-blend words: **st, sk**

Progress Check: Blends

Name_____

Read the words below. Then look at the pictures. Write the word that tells about each picture.

drum   sled   desk   flag   snake

crab   nest   plate   frog

crab

Skill: Assessment of symbol-sound association of initial **s**, **l**, and **r blends**

Vowel Pairs: AI and AY

Train has the long-a sound spelled ai. Hay has the long-a sound spelled ay.

train   hay

Read the words and look at the pictures. Circle the word that tells about each picture.

(rain) ray	train tray	mail nail
sail say	plain play	mail may
snail sail	tray trail	brain braid
rail ray	tail trail	claim clay

Skill: Symbol-sound association of words containing vowel digraphs: ai, ay

99

Vowel Pairs: EE and EA

Name_____

Bee has the long-e sound spelled **ee**. Bean has the long-e sound spelled **ea**.

bee   b**ea**n

Read the words and look at the pictures. Circle the word that tells about each picture.

see ~~seat~~	meat neat	sea seal
feet fee	beak bee	sleep seat
tea team	bee beef	jeep jeans
peas peel	heat heel	leap leaf

Review: AI, AY, EE, and EA

Name_____

Read the words and look at the pictures. Circle the word that tells about each picture.

sail say (seal) see 	pay pail peel peas	bee beat beak beef 
tail team tea tray 	mail may meat meet 	ray rain read real
play pay pain pail 	train tray rain tree 	hay heat heel hail

101

Skill: Review of symbol-sound association of words containing vowel digraphs: ai, ay, ee, ea

Vowel Pairs: OA and OW

Name_____

Coat has the long-o sound spelled **oa**.

Window has the long-o sound spelled **ow**.

c**oa**t   wind**ow**

Read the words and look at the pictures. Circle the word that tells about each picture.

boat (bowl) 	snow soap	goat grow 
crow coat	row road 	float flow 
blow bow	tow toad	crow coal 
load low 	slow snow 	oak oats 

Skill: Symbol-sound association of words containing vowel digraphs: **oa, ow**

Name_____

The sound you hear in the middle of **moon** is spelled by the letters **oo**.

m**oo**n

Name the pictures. Write **oo** below each picture whose name has the **oo** sound as in **moon**.

oo

Skill: Sound-symbol association of vowel digraphs: long **oo**

Vowel Pairs: OO

Name_____

The sound you hear in the middle of **book** is spelled by the letters **oo**.

boo**k**

Name the pictures. Write **oo** below each picture whose name has the **oo** sound, as in **book**.

oo

Skill: Sound-symbol association of vowel digraphs: short **oo**

Vowel Pairs: OO

Name_____

Read the words and name the pictures. Draw a line from each word to the picture it names.

moon   **book**

 food
foot

 pool
roof

---

 zoo
woods

 moose
hood

---

 book
boot

spoon
spool

---

 hook
stool

broom
brook

105

Skill: Symbol-sound association of words containing vowel digraphs: long and short **oo**

Review: OA, OW, and OO

Name_____

Read the words and name the pictures. Circle the word that names
each picture.

book (boat) boot bowl 	foot float flow foam	stool stood soap snow
grow good goat goal 	low look load loaf 	crow cool coal cook 
tool took tow toad	bow blow broom book	slow stoop soap spoon 

106

A Sound of Y

Name_____

The letter **y** at the end of some words can stand for the long-i sound, as in **fly**.

fly

Name the pictures. Write **y** below each picture whose name has the long-i sound, as in **fly**.

Skill: Sound-symbol association of words containing the long-i sound of **y**

A Sound of Y

Name_____

The letter **y** at the end of some words can stand for the long-**e** sound, as in **pony**.

pony

Name the pictures. Write **y** below each picture whose name has the long-**e** sound, as in **pony**.

y

20

Skill: Sound-symbol association of words containing the long-**e** sound of y

Two Sounds of Y

Name_____

Read the words and look at the pictures. Circle the word that tells about each picture.

fly   pony

---

pretty
(penny)
pry

fly
funny
fry

try
fry
cry

---

sly
spy
sky

pry
puppy
pony

by
baby
bunny

---

pry
fry
try

by
bye
baby

pony
penny
puppy

Skill: Symbol-sound association of words containing long-e and long-i sounds of y

Name_____

Read the words and name the picture. Circle the word that names each picture.

mail mow	snail snow 	try tray 
see seal 	bee by 	boat book 
soap seem 	bait boot	hair hook 
bunny bean 	stay sky 	baby by 

110

Skill: Assessment of sound-symbol association of words containing y as a vowel and of words containing vowel digraphs: **ai, ay, ee, ea, oa, ow, oo**

Consonant Pairs: SH and CH

Name_____

The sound at the beginning of **shoe** is spelled by the letters **sh**. The sound at the beginning of **chair** is spelled by the letters **ch**.

shoe   **chair**

Name the pictures. In each row, circle the picture or pictures that begin with the same sound as the first picture.

Skill: Auditory discrimination of initial consonant digraphs: **sh, ch**

Consonant Pairs: SH and CH

Name_____

Read the words below and look at the pictures.
Write the word that tells about each picture.

ship	shave	chain
sheep	chop	chin
cheek	shell	shed

shoe   **chair**

chain   _____   _____

_____   _____   _____

_____   _____   _____

112

Consonant Pairs: TH and WH

The sound at the beginning of **thin** is spelled by the letters **th**. The sound at the beginning of **wheel** is spelled by the letters **wh**.

thin   wheel

Name the pictures. In each row, circle the picture or pictures that begin with the same sound as the first picture.

30		**13**	**15**

Skill: Auditory discrimination of initial consonant digraphs: **th**, **wh**

Consonant Pairs: TH and WH

Name_____

Name the pictures. Write the letters that stand for the beginning sound of each picture name.

thin   wheel

_wh_ _____

Skill: Sound-symbol association of initial consonant digraphs: **th**, **wh**

Consonant Pairs: Final SH, CH, and TH

Name_____

The sound at the end of **wish** is spelled by the letters **sh**.

The sound at the end of **each** is spelled by the letters **ch**.

The sound at the end of **with** is spelled by the letters **th**.

w**ish**
e**ach**
w**ith**

Name the pictures. In each row, circle the picture or pictures that end with the same sound as the first picture.

			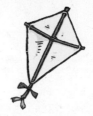

Skill: Auditory discrimination of final consonant digraphs: **sh**, **ch**, and **th**

Consonant Pairs: Final SH, CH, and TH

Name_____

Name the pictures. Write the letters that stand
for the ending sound of each picture name.

wish
each
with

_th_

Skill: Sound-symbol association of final consonant digraphs: **sh**, **ch**, and **th**

Consonant Pairs: NG

Name_____

The sound at the end of **ring** is spelled by the letters **ng**.

ri**ng**

Name the pictures. Circle each picture whose name ends with **ng**.

Skill: Auditory discrimination of final consonant digraph: **ng**

Consonant Pairs: NG

Name_____

Read the words and look at the pictures. Circle the word that tells about each picture.

ri**ng**

(swing) sing 	wing sing 	bang hang 
sting king 	sting swing 	sing bring 
song ring 	wing string 	ring king 

118

Skill: Symbol-sound association of words containing final consonant digraphs: **ng**

Review: SH, CH, TH, WH, and NG

Name _____

Read the words and look at the pictures. Circle the word that tells about each picture.

(wing) sing bring ring	chain when then shape	chin thin whip ship
math bath with path	fish dish wash push	whale shave cheese these
inch each bench beach	sheep cheap wheat that	ring wing sing swing

Skill: Review of symbol-sound association of words containing consonant
digraphs: initial **sh**, **ch**, **th**, **wh**, final **ch**, **sh**, **th**, **ng**

Progress Check: SH, CH, TH, WH, and NG

Name _____

Read the words below. Then look at the pictures. Write the word that tells about each picture.

ship	chain	thin	swing	shell
bench	wheel	brush	tooth	

chain

_____

_____

_____

_____

_____

_____

_____

_____

Skill: Assessment of symbol-sound association of words containing consonant digraphs: initial **sh**, **ch**, **th**, **wh**, final **sh**, **ch**, **th**, **ng**

Sounds and Letters

 fan

 rake

 train

 hay

 ball

 car

 chair

 dog

 bed

 bean

 bee

 fish

 goat

 horse

 bib

Sounds and Letters

 **k**it**e**

 **j**et

 **k**itten

 lion

 **m**ouse

 **n**est

 ri**ng**

 top

 **c**oat

 **b**one

 m**oo**n

 b**oo**k

 win**d**o**w**

 **p**ig

 **qu**ilt

Sounds and Letters

 rose

 sun

 shoe

 tent

 thin

 cup

 tube

 vase

 watch

 wheel

 ax

 yard

 fly

 pony

 zoo

Practice Page

Name _____

Practice Page

Name

Practice Page

Name_____

Practice Page

Name

Review: S, M, and T

Name_____

Name the pictures. Write the letter that stands for the beginning sound of each picture name.

mouse	saw	tent
m	s	t

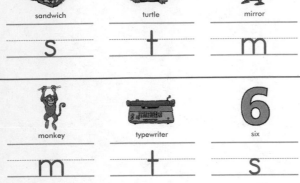

sandwich	turtle	mirror
s	t	m

monkey	typewriter	six
m	t	s

5

Ending Sounds: S, M, and T

Name_____

The sound at the end of **bus** is spelled by the letter **s**.
The sound at the end of **ham** is spelled by the letter **m**.
The sound at the end of **cat** is spelled by the letter **t**.

bus
ham
cat

Look at the pictures. Circle the letter that stands for the sound you hear at the end of the picture name.

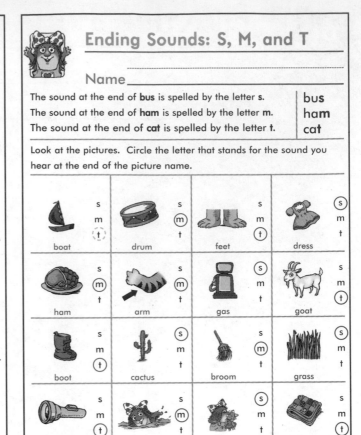

boat — s m (t)	drum — s (m) t	feet — s m (t)	dress — (s) m t
ham — s (m) t	arm — s (m) t	gas — (s) m t	goat — s m (t)
boot — s m (t)	cactus — (s) m t	broom — s (m) t	grass — (s) m t
flashlight — s m (t)	swim — s (m) t	kiss — (s) m t	quilt — s m (t)

6

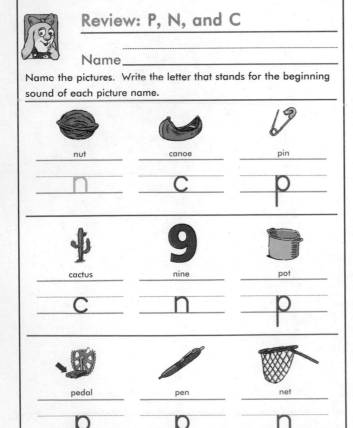

Review: P, N, and C

Name_____

Name the pictures. Write the letter that stands for the beginning sound of each picture name.

nut	canoe	pin
n	c	p

cactus	nine	pot
c	n	p

pedal	pen	net
p	p	n

7

Ending Sounds: P, N, and C

Name_____

The sound at the end of **moon** is spelled by the letter **n**.
The sound at the end of **mop** is spelled by the letter **p**.
The sound at the end of **magic** is spelled by the letter **c**.

moon
mop
magic

Name the pictures. Circle the letter that stands for the sound you hear at the end of each picture name.

ship — (p) n c	can — p (n) c	music — p n (c)	soap — (p) n c
soup — p n (c)	picnic — p n (c)	map — (p) n c	sheep — (p) n c
fan — p (n) c	cup — (p) n c	spoon — p (n) c	seven — p (n) c
mop — (p) n c	iron — p (n) c	top — (p) n c	jeep — (p) n c

8

Review: K, R, and B

Name_____

Name the pictures. Write the letter that stands for the beginning sound of each picture name.

kitten	radio	key
k	r	k

ruler	bottle	belt
r	b	b

raccoon	ring	kangaroo
r	r	k

9

Ending Sounds: K, R, and B

Name_____

The sound at the end of **book** is spelled by the letter **k**.
The sound at the end of **four** is spelled by the letter **r**.
The sound at the end of **tub** is spelled by the letter **b**.

book
four
tub

Name the pictures. Circle the letter that stands for the sound you hear at the end of each picture name.

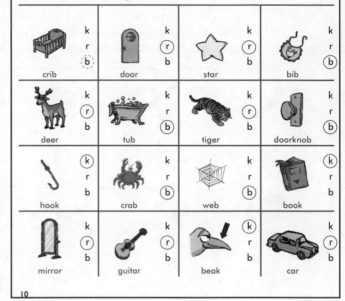

crib	k r (b)	door	k (r) b	star	k (r) b	bib	k r (b)
deer	k (r) b	tub	k r (b)	tiger	k (r) b	doorknob	k r (b)
hook	(k) r b	crab	k r (b)	web	k r (b)	book	(k) r b
mirror	k (r) b	guitar	k (r) b	beak	(k) r b	car	k (r) b

10

Review: J, F, and G

Name_____

Name the pictures. Write the letter that stands for the beginning sound of each picture name.

fan	jar	football
f	j	f

guitar	four	jeep
g	f	j

five	game	jacket
f	g	j

11

Ending Sounds: F and G

Name_____

The sound at the end of **roof** is spelled by the letter **f**.
The sound at the end of **bag** is spelled by the letter **g**.

roof
bag

Name the pictures. Circle the letter that stands for the sound you hear at the end of each picture name.

bag	f (g)	egg	f (g)	leaf	(f) g	tag	f (g)
scarf	(f) g	pig	f (g)	flag	f (g)	frog	f (g)
wig	f (g)	rug	f (g)	log	f (g)	roof	(f) g
ladybug	f (g)	hoof	(f) g	leg	f (g)	dog	f (g)

12

129

Review: H, D, and Z

Name_____

Name the pictures. Write the letter that stands for the beginning sound of each picture name.

hammer	deer	hook
h	d	h

zipper	doll	door
z	d	d

hose	zero	dog
h	z	d

13

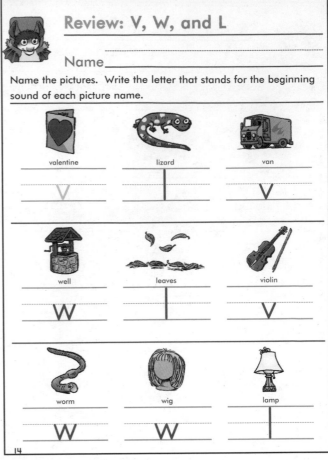

Review: V, W, and L

Name_____

Name the pictures. Write the letter that stands for the beginning sound of each picture name.

valentine	lizard	van
v	l	v

well	leaves	violin
w	l	v

worm	wig	lamp
w	w	l

14

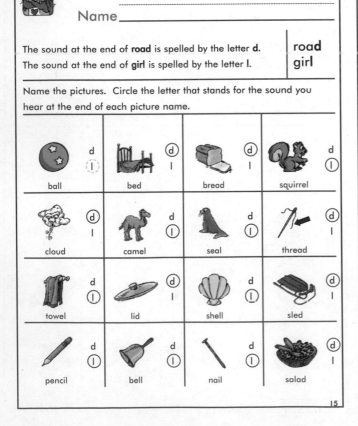

Ending Sounds: D and L

Name_____

The sound at the end of **road** is spelled by the letter **d**.
The sound at the end of **girl** is spelled by the letter **l**.

road
girl

Name the pictures. Circle the letter that stands for the sound you hear at the end of each picture name.

ball	d / (l)	bed	(d) / l	bread	(d) / l	squirrel	d / (l)
cloud	(d) / l	camel	d / (l)	seal	d / (l)	thread	(d) / l
towel	d / (l)	lid	(d) / l	shell	d / (l)	sled	(d) / l
pencil	d / (l)	bell	d / (l)	nail	d / (l)	salad	(d) / l

15

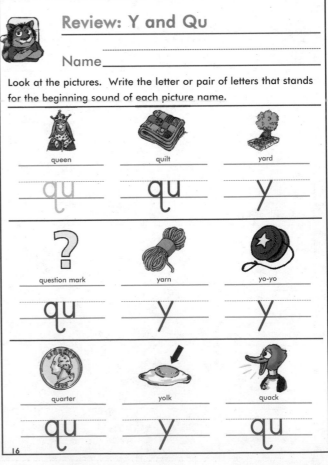

Review: Y and Qu

Name_____

Look at the pictures. Write the letter or pair of letters that stands for the beginning sound of each picture name.

queen	quilt	yard
qu	qu	y

question mark	yarn	yo-yo
qu	y	y

quarter	yolk	quack
qu	y	qu

16

130

Review: Ending Sounds

Name_____

Name the pictures. Write the letter that stands for the ending sound of each picture name.

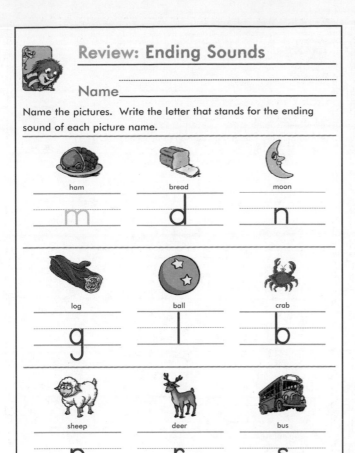

ham — m
bread — d
moon — n

log — g
ball — l
crab — b

sheep — p
deer — r
bus — s

17

Progress Check: Consonants

Name_____

Name the pictures. Write the letters that stand for the beginning and ending sounds of each picture name.

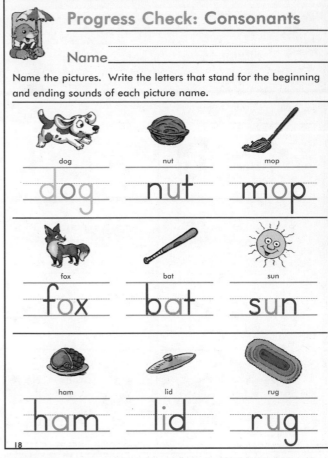

dog — dog
nut — nut
mop — mop

fox — fox
bat — bat
sun — sun

ham — ham
lid — lid
rug — rug

18

Short A

Name_____

Fan has the short-**a** sound. This sound is usually spelled by the letter **a**.

fan

Name the pictures. Circle each picture whose name has the short-**a** sound.

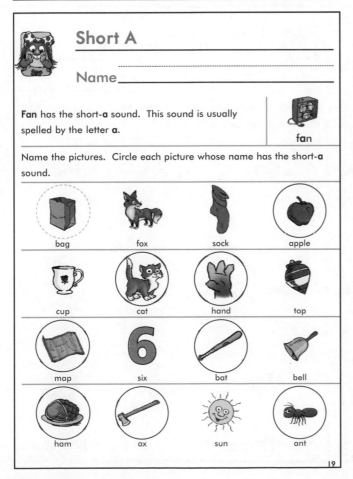

bag, fox, sock, apple
cup, cat, hand, top
map, six, bat, bell
ham, ax, sun, ant

19

Short A

Name_____

Name the pictures. Write **a** below each picture whose name has the short-**a** sound.

fan

man — a
lamp — a
vest

ax — a
pig
bat — a

candle
basket
clock

a

20

131

Short A

Name

Read the words and name the pictures. Draw a line from each word to the picture it names.

fan

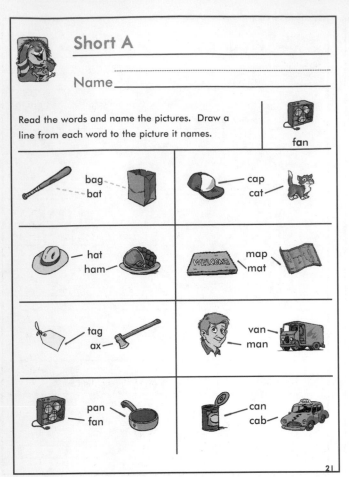

bag	cap
bat	cat
hat	map
ham	mat
tag	van
ax	man
pan	can
fan	cab

21

Short A

Name

Read each sentence and the words beside it.
Write the word that makes sense in each sentence.

fan

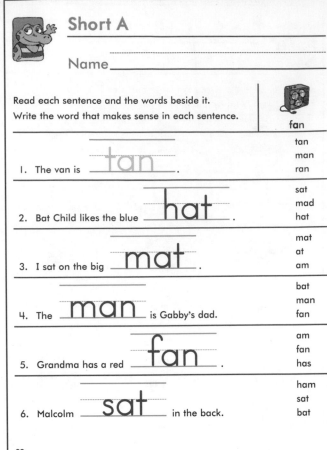

1. The van is ___tan___ .
   - tan
   - man
   - ran

2. Bat Child likes the blue ___hat___ .
   - sat
   - mad
   - hat

3. I sat on the big ___mat___ .
   - mat
   - at
   - am

4. The ___man___ is Gabby's dad.
   - bat
   - man
   - fan

5. Grandma has a red ___fan___ .
   - am
   - fan
   - has

6. Malcolm ___sat___ in the back.
   - ham
   - sat
   - bat

22

Short I

Name

Bib has the short-i sound. This sound is usually spelled by the letter **i**.

bib

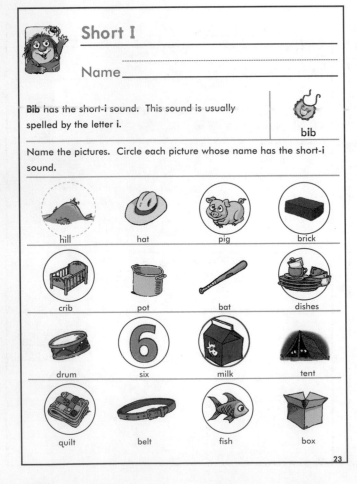

Name the pictures. Circle each picture whose name has the short-**i** sound.

hill	hat	pig	brick
crib	pot	bat	dishes
drum	six	milk	tent
quilt	belt	fish	box

23

Short I

Name

Name the pictures. Write **i** below each picture whose name has the short-i sound.

bib

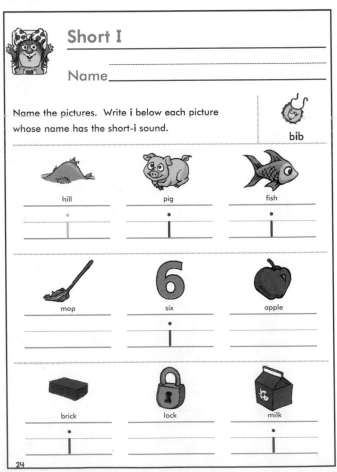

hill	pig	fish
i	i	i
mop	six	apple
	i	
brick	lock	milk
i	i	i

24

132

Short I

Name

Read the words and look at the pictures. Draw a line from each word to the picture it tells about.

bib

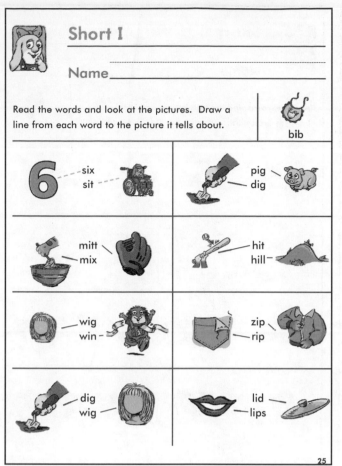

six
sit

pig
dig

mitt
mix

hit
hill

wig
win

zip
rip

dig
wig

lid
lips

25

Short I

Name

Read each sentence and the words beside it. Write the word that makes sense in each sentence.

bib

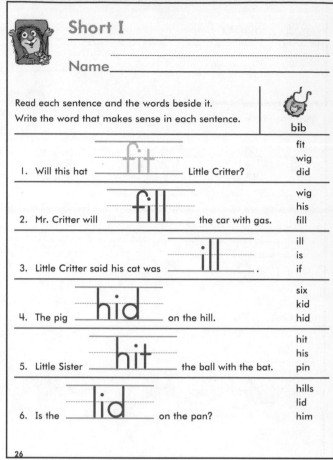

1. Will this hat ___fit___ Little Critter?
   - fit
   - wig
   - did

2. Mr. Critter will ___fill___ the car with gas.
   - wig
   - his
   - fill

3. Little Critter said his cat was ___ill___ .
   - ill
   - is
   - if

4. The pig ___hid___ on the hill.
   - six
   - kid
   - hid

5. Little Sister ___hit___ the ball with the bat.
   - hit
   - his
   - pin

6. Is the ___lid___ on the pan?
   - hills
   - lid
   - him

26

Review: Short A and I

Name

Read the words and look at the pictures. Circle the word that tells about each picture.

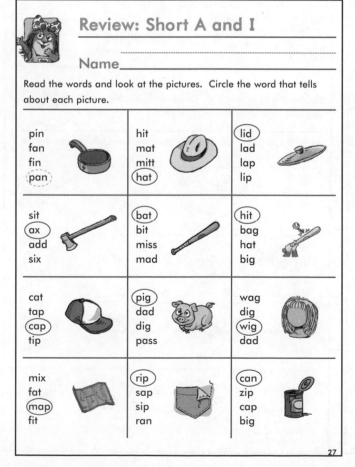

pin fan fin (pan)	hit mat mitt (hat)	(lid) lad lap lip
sit (ax) add six	(bat) bit miss mad	(hit) bag hat big
cat tap (cap) tip	(pig) dad dig pass	wag dig (wig) dad
mix fat (map) fit	(rip) sap sip ran	(can) zip cap big

27

Short O

Name

Top has the short-o sound. This sound is usually spelled by the letter **o**.

top

Name the pictures. Circle each picture whose name has the short-o sound.

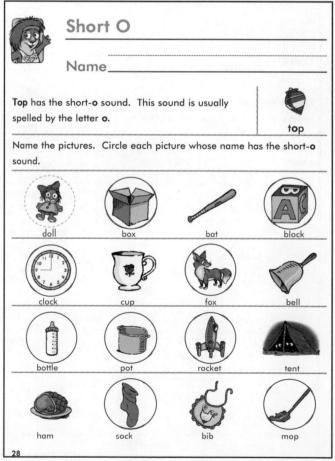

doll	box	bat	block
clock	cup	fox	bell
bottle	pot	rocket	tent
ham	sock	bib	mop

28

133

Short O

Name

Name the pictures. Write **o** below each picture whose name has the short-o sound.

top

block	fox	cat
	o	o

cup	ten	clock
		o

mop	clock	ant
o	o	

29

Short O

Name

Read the words and look at the pictures. Draw a line from each word to the picture it tells about.

top

box
fox

doll
dots

cob
cot

hot
hop

pop
pot

mop
rod

ox
top

hog
log

30

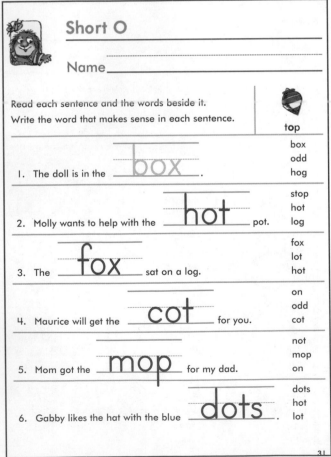

Short O

Name

Read each sentence and the words beside it.
Write the word that makes sense in each sentence.

top

1. The doll is in the __box__ .
   box
   odd
   hog

2. Molly wants to help with the __hot__ pot.
   stop
   hot
   log

3. The __fox__ sat on a log.
   fox
   lot
   hot

4. Maurice will get the __cot__ for you.
   on
   odd
   cot

5. Mom got the __mop__ for my dad.
   not
   mop
   on

6. Gabby likes the hat with the blue __dots__ .
   dots
   hot
   lot

31

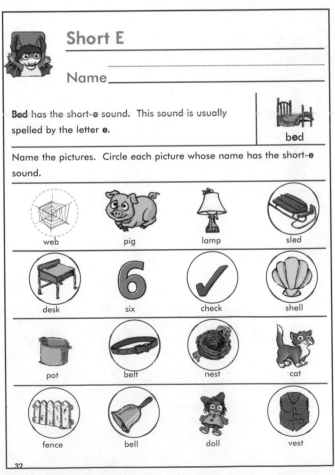

Short E

Name

Bed has the short-**e** sound. This sound is usually spelled by the letter **e**.

bed

Name the pictures. Circle each picture whose name has the short-e sound.

web	pig	lamp	sled

desk	six	check	shell

pot	belt	nest	cat

fence	bell	doll	vest

32

134

Short E

Name_____

Name the pictures. Write **e** below each picture whose name has the short-**e** sound.

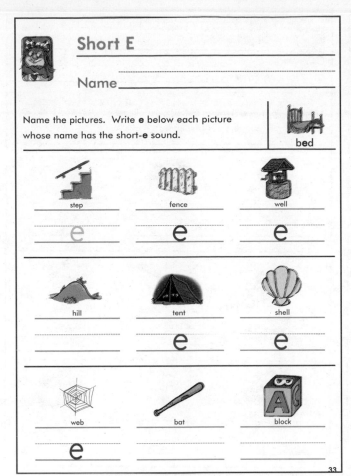

bed

step	fence	well
e	e	e

hill	tent	shell
	e	e

web	bat	block
e		

33

Short E

Name_____

Read the words and look at the pictures. Draw a line from each word to the picture it tells about.

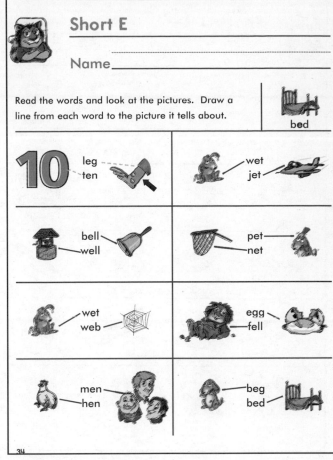

bed

10   leg   ten

wet   jet

bell   well

pet   net

wet   web

egg   fell

men   hen

beg   bed

34

Short E

Name_____

Read each sentence and the words beside it. Write the word that makes sense in each sentence.

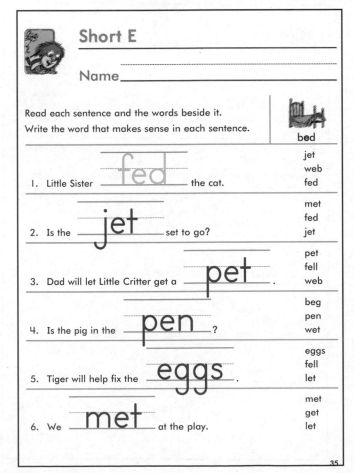

bed

1. Little Sister ___fed___ the cat.

         jet
         web
         fed

2. Is the ___jet___ set to go?

         met
         fed
         jet

3. Dad will let Little Critter get a ___pet___ .

         pet
         fell
         web

4. Is the pig in the ___pen___ ?

         beg
         pen
         wet

5. Tiger will help fix the ___eggs___ .

         eggs
         fell
         let

6. We ___met___ at the play.

         met
         get
         let

35

Review: Short O and E

Name_____

Read the words and look at the pictures. Circle the word that tells about each picture.

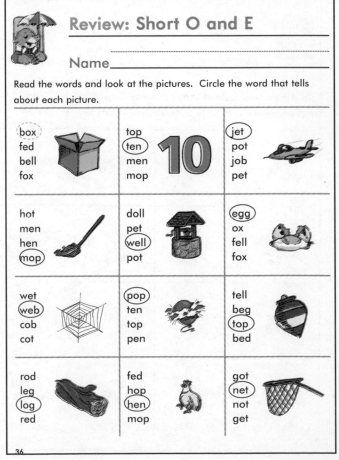

(box) fed bell fox	top (ten) men mop **10**	(jet) pot job pet
hot men hen (mop)	doll pet (well) pot	(egg) ox fell fox
wet (web) cob cot	(pop) ten top pen	tell beg (top) bed
rod leg (log) red	fed hop (hen) mop	got (net) not get

36

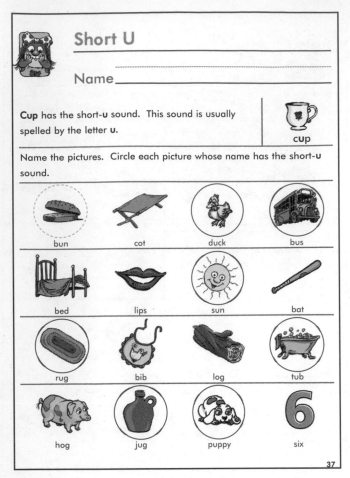

Short U

Name _____

Cup has the short-**u** sound. This sound is usually spelled by the letter **u**.

cup

Name the pictures. Circle each picture whose name has the short-**u** sound.

bun	cot	duck	bus
bed	lips	sun	bat
rug	bib	log	tub
hog	jug	puppy	six

37

Short U

Name _____

Name the pictures. Write **u** below each picture whose name has the short-**u** sound.

cup

hug	tent	sun
u		u
rug	ax	jug
u		u
fish	duck	bus
	u	u

38

Short U

Name _____

Read the words and look at the pictures. Draw a line from each word to the picture it tells about.

cup

bus
sun

bun
bug

tub
hug

run
rug

cup
pup

cut
cub

mud
mug

nut
jug

39

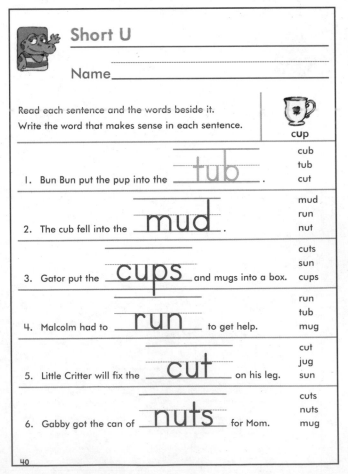

Short U

Name _____

Read each sentence and the words beside it. Write the word that makes sense in each sentence.

cup

1. Bun Bun put the pup into the __tub__ .

cub
tub
cut

2. The cub fell into the __mud__ .

mud
run
nut

3. Gator put the __cups__ and mugs into a box.

cuts
sun
cups

4. Malcolm had to __run__ to get help.

run
tub
mug

5. Little Critter will fix the __cut__ on his leg.

cut
jug
sun

6. Gabby got the can of __nuts__ for Mom.

cuts
nuts
mug

40

136

Review: Short Vowels

Name_____

Read the words and name the pictures. Circle the word that names each picture.

(sun) suds sad sat		lid lad lip lap		(mug) mal man mud	
(cat) cob cab cot		bag (bed) bad beg		pin pen peg (pig)	
ran (rug) rag rub		bit beg bet (bib)		(net) nut men met	
top tab (tub) tap		but (bat) bit bet		bug but bun (bus)	

41

Short Vowels

Name_____

Name the pictures. Circle the letter that stands for the vowel sound in each picture name. Then write the letter to complete the picture name.

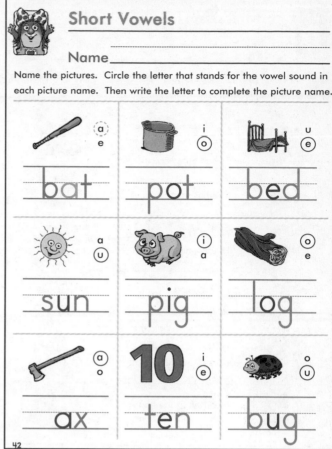

(a) e	i (o)	u (e)
bat	pot	bed
a (u)	(i) a	(o) e
sun	pig	log
(a) o	i (e)	o (u)
ax	ten	bug

42

Short Vowels

Name_____

Circle the word that names each picture. Then write the word in the blank.

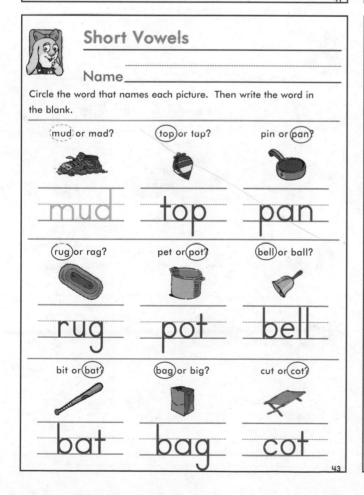

(mud) or mad? (top) or tap? pin or (pan)?

mud   top   pan

(rug) or rag? pet or (pot)? (bell) or ball?

rug   pot   bell

bit or (bat)? (bag) or big? cut or (cot)?

bat   bag   cot

43

Short Vowels

Name_____

Read the sentences and the words under the blanks. Circle the word that belongs in each sentence. Then write the word in the blank.

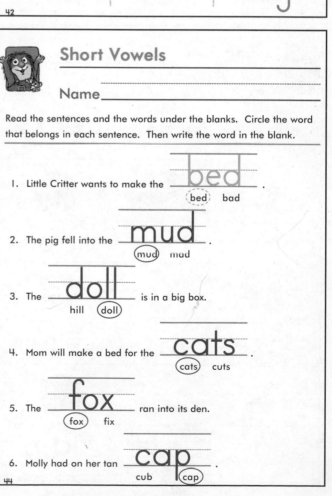

1. Little Critter wants to make the ___bed___ .
   (bed) bad

2. The pig fell into the ___mud___ .
   (mud) mad

3. The ___doll___ is in a big box.
   hill (doll)

4. Mom will make a bed for the ___cats___ .
   (cats) cuts

5. The ___fox___ ran into its den.
   (fox) fix

6. Molly had on her tan ___cap___ .
   cub (cap)

44

Short Vowels

Name_____

Read the sentences and look at the pictures. Draw a line from each sentence to the picture it tells about.

The cat plays with the rag.
The cat plays with the rug.

Dad has the mop.
Dad has the map.

The dog has the bell.
The dog has the ball.

Little Sister got the bug.
Little Sister got the bag.

Little Critter has a red cup.
Little Critter has a red cap.

Mom will fix the ham.
Mom will fix the hem.

45

Long A

Name_____

Rake has the long-**a** sound. This sound is often spelled by **a** and silent **e**.

rake

Name the pictures. Circle each picture whose name has the long-**a** sound.

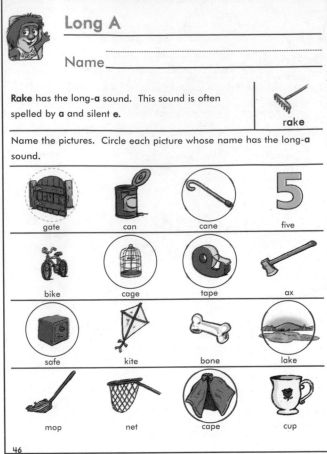

gate   can   cane   five

bike   cage   tape   ax

safe   kite   bone   lake

mop   net   cape   cup

46

Long A

Name_____

Name the pictures. Write the letter or letters to complete each picture name.

fan   rake

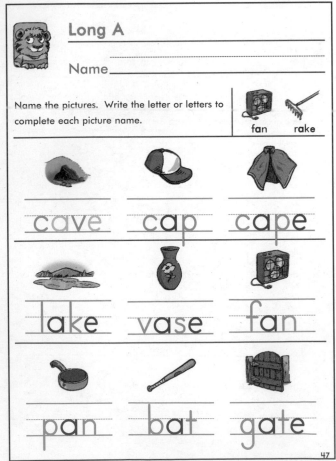

cave   cap   cape

lake   vase   fan

pan   bat   gate

47

Long A

Name_____

Read the words and name the pictures. Draw a line from each word to the picture it names.

fan   rake

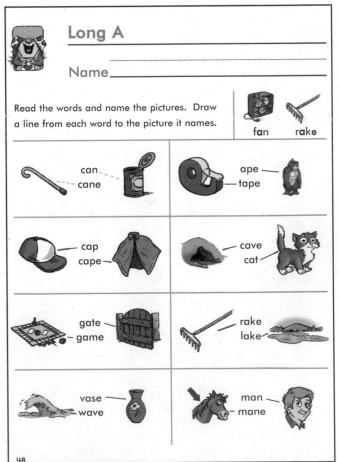

can
cane

ape
tape

cap
cape

cave
cat

gate
game

rake
lake

vase
wave

man
mane

48

138

Long A

Name_____

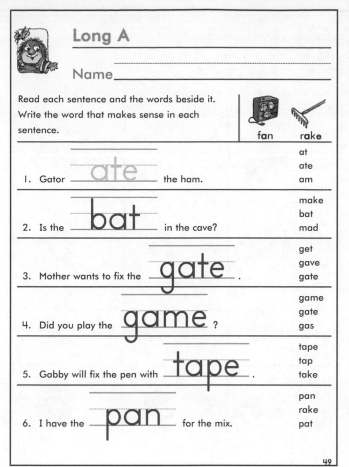

Read each sentence and the words beside it. Write the word that makes sense in each sentence.

| fan | rake |

1. Gator ___ate___ the ham.
   - at
   - ate
   - am

2. Is the ___bat___ in the cave?
   - make
   - bat
   - mad

3. Mother wants to fix the ___gate___.
   - get
   - gave
   - gate

4. Did you play the ___game___?
   - game
   - gate
   - gas

5. Gabby will fix the pen with ___tape___.
   - tape
   - tap
   - take

6. I have the ___pan___ for the mix.
   - pan
   - rake
   - pat

49

Long I

Name_____

Kite has the long-i sound. This sound is often spelled by **i** and silent **e**.

kite

Name the pictures. Circle each picture whose name has the long-i sound.

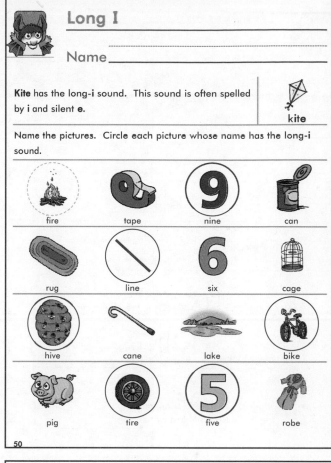

fire   tape   nine   can

rug   line   six   cage

hive   cane   lake   bike

pig   tire   five   robe

50

Long I

Name_____

Read the words and look at the pictures. Draw a line from each word to the picture it tells about.

bib   kite

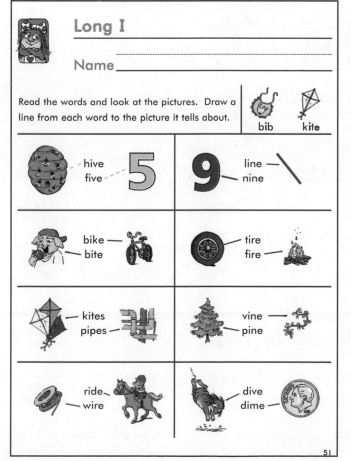

hive
five   5

9   line
nine

bike
bite

tire
fire

kites
pipes

vine
pine

ride
wire

dive
dime

51

Long I

Name_____

Name the pictures. Write the letter or letters to complete each picture name.

bib   kite

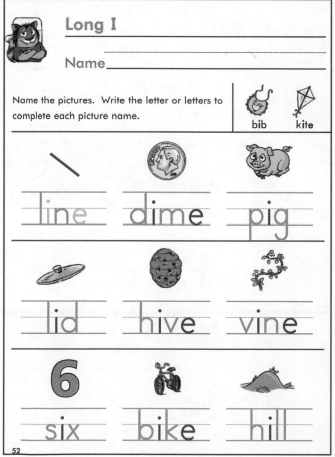

line   dime   pig

lid   hive   vine

six   bike   hill

52

139

Long I

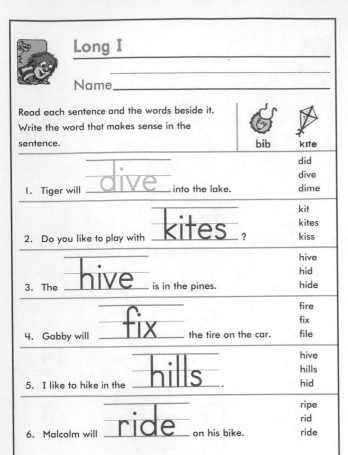

Name_____

Read each sentence and the words beside it. Write the word that makes sense in the sentence.

	bib	kite

1. Tiger will **dive** into the lake.

	did
	dive
	dime

2. Do you like to play with **kites** ?

	kit
	kites
	kiss

3. The **hive** is in the pines.

	hive
	hid
	hide

4. Gabby will **fix** the tire on the car.

	fire
	fix
	file

5. I like to hike in the **hills**.

	hive
	hills
	hid

6. Malcolm will **ride** on his bike.

	ripe
	rid
	ride

53

Review: Long A and Long I

Name_____

Read the words and look at the pictures. Circle the word that tells about each picture.

time tin tap (tape)	kit can kite (cane)	dim (dime) date dam
pan (van) vine pine	bit (bike) bite big	(ride) rat ran rid
hide (hive) hat hate	miss (mat) mitt man	(dive) dad did date
lad lid like (lake)	sat side (safe) sit	(pine) pin pal pale

54

Long O

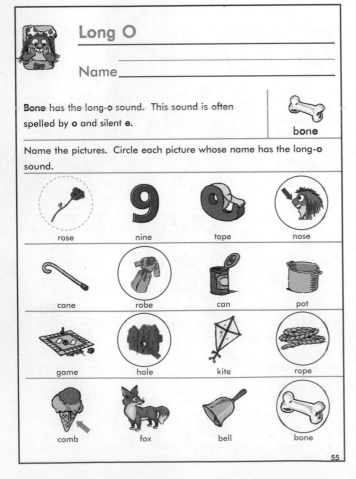

Name_____

Bone has the long-o sound. This sound is often spelled by **o** and silent **e**.

	bone

Name the pictures. Circle each picture whose name has the long-o sound.

rose   nine   tape   nose

cane   robe   can   pot

game   hole   kite   rope

comb   fox   bell   bone

55

Long O

Name_____

Read the words and look at the pictures. Draw a line from each word to the picture it tells about.

	top	bone

rope   vote | poke   pot

home   hop | cone   bone

note   robe | hose   hole

pole   pop | rose   nose

56

140

Long O

Name_____

Name the pictures. Write the letter or letters to complete each picture name.

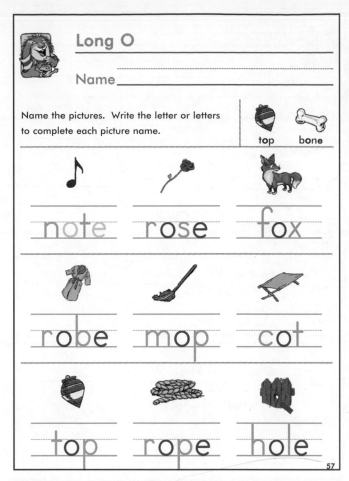

| | top | bone |

note   rose   fox

robe   mop   cot

top   rope   hole

57

Long O

Name_____

Read each sentence and the words beside it. Write the word that makes sense in the sentence.

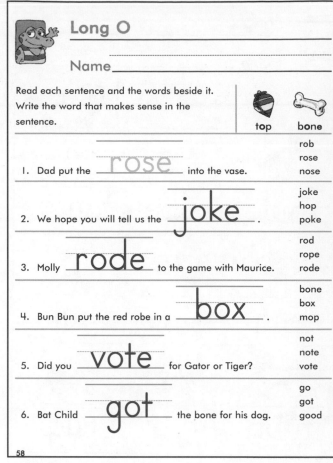

| | top | bone |

1. Dad put the __rose__ into the vase.

| rob |
| rose |
| nose |

2. We hope you will tell us the __joke__ .

| joke |
| hop |
| poke |

3. Molly __rode__ to the game with Maurice.

| rod |
| rope |
| rode |

4. Bun Bun put the red robe in a __box__ .

| bone |
| box |
| mop |

5. Did you __vote__ for Gator or Tiger?

| not |
| note |
| vote |

6. Bat Child __got__ the bone for his dog.

| go |
| got |
| good |

58

Long U

Name_____

Tube has the long-**u** sound. This sound is often spelled by **u** and silent **e**.

| tube |

Name the pictures. Circle each picture whose name has the long-**u** sound.

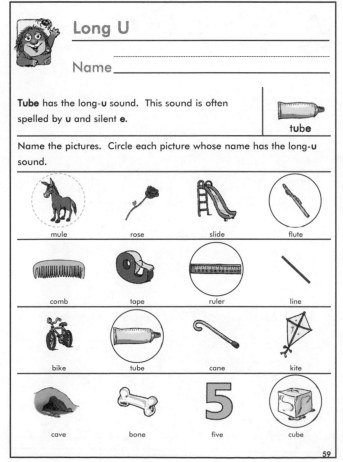

mule	rose	slide	flute
comb	tape	ruler	line
bike	tube	cane	kite
cave	bone	five	cube

59

Long U

Name_____

Read the words and look at the pictures. Draw a line from each word to the picture it tells about.

| cup | tube |

mud / mule	rug / mug
cub / cube	run / ruler
cut / cute	tune / bun
tub / tube	bus / bug

60

141

Long U

Name_____

Look at each picture. Write the letter or letters to complete the word that tells about the picture.

cup   tube

mule   cube   cup

bug   tune   cut

tube   tub   rug

61

Long U

Name_____

Read each sentence and the words beside it. Write the word that makes sense in each sentence.

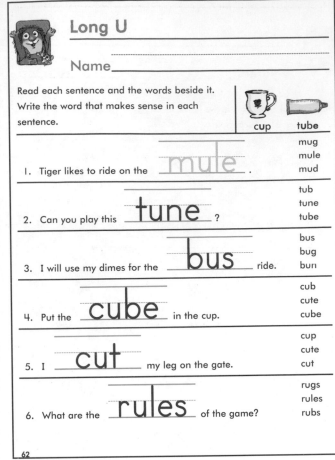

cup   tube

1. Tiger likes to ride on the __mule__ .		mug / mule / mud
2. Can you play this __tune__ ?		tub / tune / tube
3. I will use my dimes for the __bus__ ride.		bus / bug / bun
4. Put the __cube__ in the cup.		cub / cute / cube
5. I __cut__ my leg on the gate.		cup / cute / cut
6. What are the __rules__ of the game?		rugs / rules / rubs

62

Review: Long O and Long U

Name_____

Read the words and name the pictures. Circle the word that names each picture.

cub	rode	top
cob	(ruler)	toss
(cone)	rod	tube
(cube)	run	(tub)
(mop)	note	(mule)
mug	(nut)	mug
mole	not	moss
mule	nose	mole
rule	bone	(top)
(rose)	but	tune
rod	(bus)	tug
rug	box	tone
rule	(bone)	(note)
run	box	nut
(rope)	bus	nose
rot	bun	not

63

Review: Long Vowels

Name_____

Name the pictures. Write the letters to complete each picture name.

hive   rope   tube

note   mule   cube

bone   vine   lake

64

142

Long Vowels

Name_____

Read each sentence and the words beside it. Write the word that makes sense in the sentence.

1. Nine bats are in the __cave__ .	cave
	came
	note
2. I may __make__ a cape.	vote
	make
	kite
3. What is his __name__ ?	name
	five
	nine
4. The lid is on the __tube__ .	time
	tune
	tube
5. Did you __dive__ into the lake?	dive
	hive
	live
6. The puppy wants to __hide__ the bone.	line
	hope
	hide

65

Long Vowels

Name_____

Circle the word that tells about each picture. Then write the word in the blank.

dive or date?	cube or cape?	cone or cane?
dive	cape	cane
rode or rope?	cute or cave?	line or lake?
rope	cute	lake
rake or rope?	time or tape?	ride or rose?
rake	time	rose

66

Long Vowels

Name_____

Read the sentences and name the pictures. Write the word that names each picture.

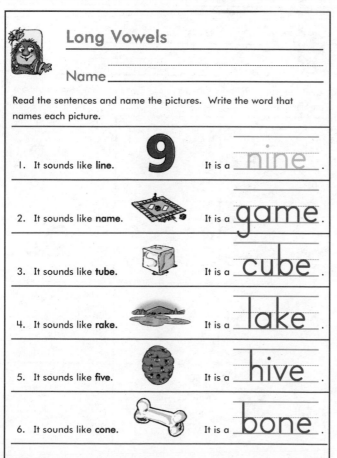

1. It sounds like **line**.   **9**   It is a __nine__ .

2. It sounds like **name**.   It is a __game__ .

3. It sounds like **tube**.   It is a __cube__ .

4. It sounds like **rake**.   It is a __lake__ .

5. It sounds like **five**.   It is a __hive__ .

6. It sounds like **cone**.   It is a __bone__ .

67

Long Vowels

Name_____

Read the words below. Then name the pictures. Write the word that names each picture.

nine	tube	note
wave	rake	hive
bone	bike	cube

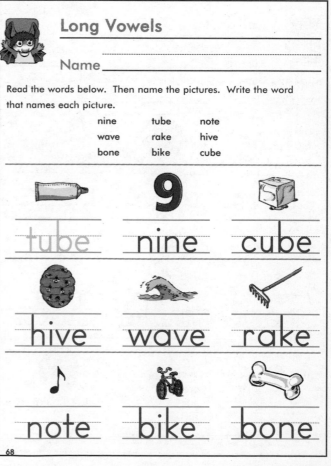

tube	nine	cube
hive	wave	rake
note	bike	bone

68

143

Long Vowels

Name_____

Look at each picture. Circle the letters that stand for the vowel sound. Then write the letters to complete the word that tells about the picture.

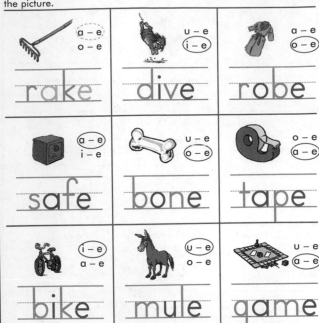

	a – e		u – e		a – e
	(o – e)		(i – e)		(o – e)
rake		dive		robe	

	(a – e)		u – e		o – e
	i – e		(o – e)		(a – e)
safe		bone		tape	

	(i – e)		(u – e)		u – e
	a – e		o – e		(a – e)
bike		mule		game	

69

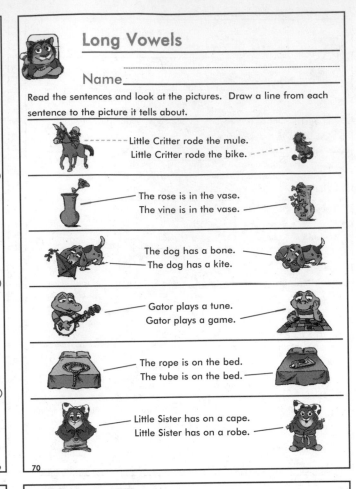

Long Vowels

Name_____

Read the sentences and look at the pictures. Draw a line from each sentence to the picture it tells about.

Little Critter rode the mule.
Little Critter rode the bike.

The rose is in the vase.
The vine is in the vase.

The dog has a bone.
The dog has a kite.

Gator plays a tune.
Gator plays a game.

The rope is on the bed.
The tube is on the bed.

Little Sister has on a cape.
Little Sister has on a robe.

70

Long Vowels

Name_____

Name the pictures. Write the letters to complete each picture name.

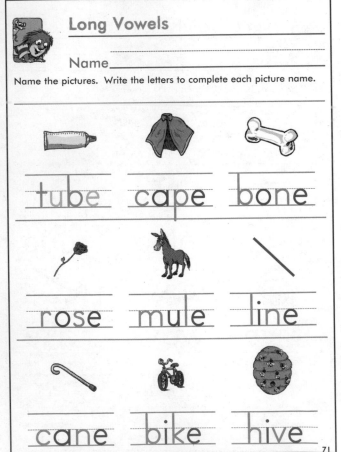

tube	cape	bone
rose	mule	line
cane	bike	hive

71

Long Vowels

Name_____

Read the words and name the pictures. Circle the word that names each picture.

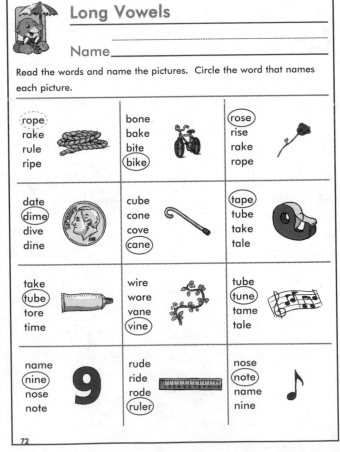

(rope) rake rule ripe	bone bake bite (bike)	(rose) rise rake rope
date (dime) dive dine	cube cone cove (cane)	(tape) tube take tale
take (tube) tore time	wire wore vane (vine)	tube (tune) tame tale
name (nine) nose note	rude ride rode (ruler)	nose (note) name nine

72

144

Short and Long Vowels

Name_____

Name the pictures. Write the letter or letters to complete each picture name.

vine   rose   lake

web   five   fox

mule   bib   ten

73

Short and Long Vowels

Name_____

Read the words and name the pictures. Draw lines from the words to the pictures they name.

 pan pale pad   nose not note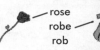

 cat cave came   rose robe rob

 bike bib bite   cube cut cub

 man mane map   pine pig pin

74

Short and Long Vowels

Name_____

Read each sentence and the words beside it. Write the word that makes sense in each sentence.

1. Did you ride the ___bike___ ?
     bit / bite / bike

2. Put on the red ___robe___ .
     rob / rug / robe

3. Tell Little Critter to ___fix___ the kite.
     fix / fox / five

4. I have ___nine___ dimes to save.
     net / nine / name

5. The ___fox___ ran into the den.
     fat / fox / fine

6. Put the ___lid___ on the pot.
     lid / like / line

75

Short and Long Vowels

Name_____

Read the sentences and name the pictures. Write the word that names each picture.

1. It sounds like **bite**. It is a __kite__ .

2. It sounds like **fan**. It is a __pan__ .

3. It sounds like **cot**. It is a __pot__ .

4. It sounds like **red**. It is a __bed__ .

5. It sounds like **nose**. It is a __rose__ .

6. It sounds like **save**. It is a __cave__ .

76

145

Short and Long Vowels

Name _____

Read the words below. Then name the pictures. Write the word that names each picture.

nine	rose	bat
pig	hive	cube
box	cane	sun

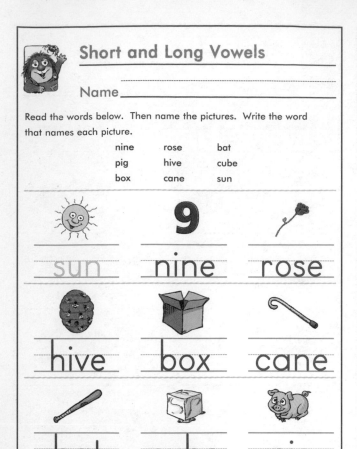

sun   nine   rose

hive   box   cane

bat   cube   pig

77

Short and Long Vowels

Name _____

Read the sentences and look at the pictures. Draw a line from each sentence to the picture it tells about.

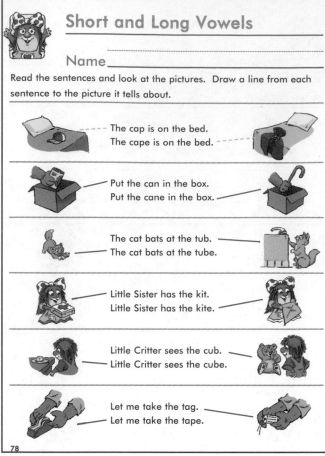

The cap is on the bed.
The cape is on the bed.

Put the can in the box.
Put the cane in the box.

The cat bats at the tub.
The cat bats at the tube.

Little Sister has the kit.
Little Sister has the kite.

Little Critter sees the cub.
Little Critter sees the cube.

Let me take the tag.
Let me take the tape.

78

Progress Check: Short and Long Vowels

Name _____

Name each picture. Write the letter or letters to complete the word that names the picture.

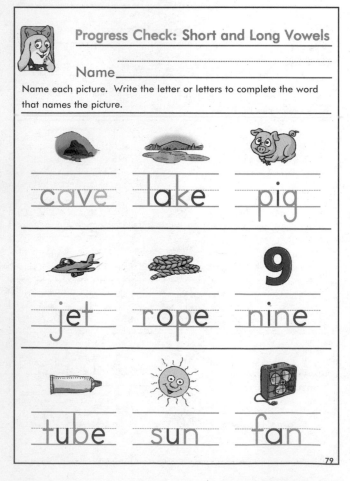

cave   lake   pig

jet   rope   nine

tube   sun   fan

79

S Blends

Name _____

In some words, the letter **s** comes before another consonant. To say these words, blend the sound of **s** with the sound of the consonant that follows it.

stop	skate
smile	sleep

Look at the pictures. In each row, circle the picture or pictures that begin with the same sound as the first picture.

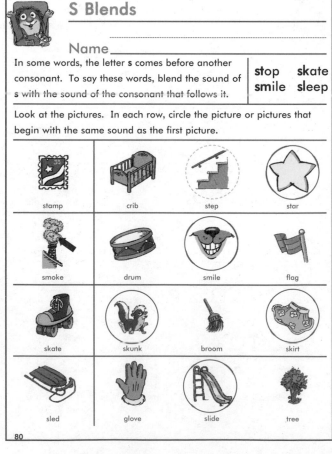

stamp	crib	step	star
smoke	drum	smile	flag
skate	skunk	broom	skirt
sled	glove	slide	tree

80

146

S Blends

Name_____

Read the words below. Then look at the pictures. Write the word that tells about each picture.

sled	skip	step	smoke	stem
skate	stone	slide	smile	

stem   sled   smile

skate   slide   skip

step   smoke   stone

81

S Blends

Name_____

In some words, the letter **s** comes before another consonant. To say these words, blend the sound of **s** with the sound of the consonant that follows it.

scare	snap
swim	spin

Look at the pictures. In each row, circle the picture or pictures that begin with the same sound as the first picture.

spider	spaghetti	spoon	grill
sweater	swan	bread	sweep
scarecrow	tree	scarf	fly
snake	snow	frog	snail

82

S Blends

Name_____

Read the words below. Then look at the pictures. Write the word that tells about each picture.

spill	snake	scale	snip	spell
snap	scare	swim	spin	

scare   snip   scale

spill   snake   swim

spin   spell   snap

83

Review: S Blends

Name_____

Read the words and look at the pictures. Circle the word that tells about each picture.

slim (skip) snip swim		(smell) swell spell still		spine smile skid (slide)	
spoke (stone) smoke slope		(swim) slim spin skin		stop slap skip (snap)	
(spill) swell smell still		snake state (scale) spare		(spin) skin slim swim	

84

147

L Blends

Name_____

In some words, the letter l follows another consonant. To say these words, blend the sound of the first consonant with the sound of l.

flower
play

Name the pictures. In each row, circle the picture or pictures that begin with the same sound as the first picture.

flower	flag	truck	fly
plant	skunk	playground	scarf
flashlight	brush	flute	flower
plate	pliers	tree	plow

85

L Blends

Name_____

Read the words below. Then look at the pictures. Write the word that tells about each picture.

play   plate   flag   flute   plane
plug   flame   flat   plum

flute	flag	plate
flame	play	plug
plum	plane	flat

86

L Blends

Name_____

In some words, the letter l follows another consonant. To say these words, blend the sound of the first consonant with the sound of l.

clown
blue
glad

Look at the pictures. In each row, circle the picture or pictures that begin with the same sound as the first picture.

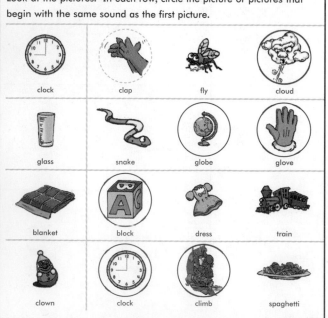

clock	clap	fly	cloud
glass	snake	globe	glove
blanket	block	dress	train
clown	clock	climb	spaghetti

87

L Blends

Name_____

Read the words below. Then look at the pictures. Write the word that tells about each picture.

clip   blade   globe   clam   glass
club   clap   class   glad

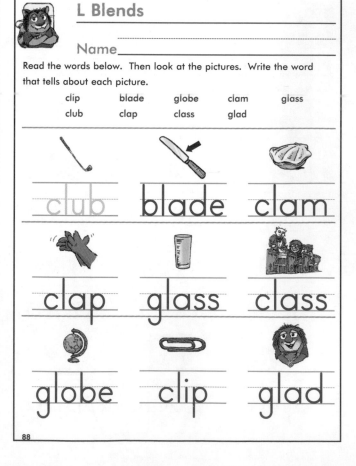

club	blade	clam
clap	glass	class
globe	clip	glad

88

148

Review: L Blends

Name_____

Read the words and name the pictures. Circle the word that names each picture.

(clip) flap glad plan	clap blaze (glass) flame	(flute) plate blade glad
glare plane flame (blade)	(plane) flake blame clam	play (clap) flag glad
club plug (flag) glad	flake (plate) blame glare	(globe) blob club plug

89

R Blends

Name_____

In some words, the letter **r** follows another consonant. To say these words, blend the sound of the first consonant with the sound of **r**.

frog brown green

Name the pictures. In each row, circle the pictures that begin with the same sound as the first picture.

frog	fruit	spoon	frame
broom	squirrel	brick	brush
grass	grill	grapes	dress
bread	bridge	bracelet	fly

90

R Blends

Name_____

Read the words below. Then look at the pictures. Write the word that tells about each picture.

grab   frog   bride   grade   grape
grill   grin   frame   graze

bride   grin   grade

grab   grape   graze

grill   frog   frame

91

R Blends

Name_____

In some words, the letter **r** follows another consonant. To say these words, blend the sound of the first consonant with the sound of **r**.

**cry   pretty
dress   tree**

Look at the pictures. In each row, circle the picture or pictures that begin with the same sound as the first picture.

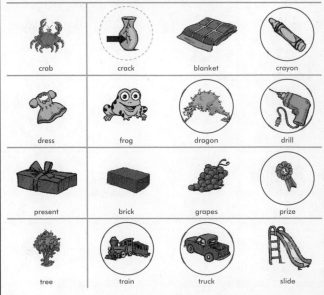

crab	crack	blanket	crayon
dress	frog	dragon	drill
present	brick	grapes	prize
tree	train	truck	slide

92

149

R Blends

Name_____

Read the words below. Then look at the pictures. Write the word that tells about each picture.

trip	trap	crib	drip	crab
dress	drill	drum	prize	

drip   crib   trip

trap   drill   prize

dress   crab   drum

93

Review: R Blends

Name_____

Read the words and look at the pictures. Circle the word that tells about each picture.

grapes		from		grill	
brave		drum		drip	
trade		grab		crib	
frames		crate		trap	
crab		prize		drag	
grass		bride		frog	
trap		drive		crop	
drag		trade		grab	
prize		grin		graze	
bride		trim		prize	
froze		drum		prune	
drive		from		bride	

94

Final S Blends

Name_____

At the end of some words, the letter **s** comes before another consonant. To say these words, blend the sound of **s** with the sound of that consonant.

ask
just

Look at the pictures. In each row, circle the picture or pictures that end with the same sound as the first picture.

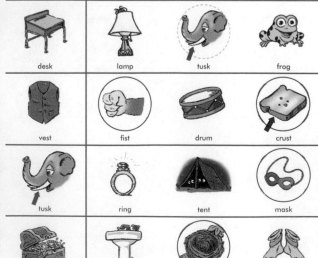

95

Final S Blends

Name_____

Read the words below. Then look at the pictures. Write the word that tells about each picture.

list	nest	fist
mask	cast	desk
crust	vest	tusk

vest   mask   fist

crust   cast   nest

tusk   list   desk

96

150

Review: Final S Blends

Name_____

Read the words and look at the pictures. Circle the word that tells about each picture.

test nest task (tusk)		cast (crust) dust desk		(list) last test tusk	
cost (cast) mask most		pest (nest) must mask		most desk dust (mask)	
tusk test (vest) most		(desk) ask mask must		fast task (fist) tusk	

97

Progress Check: Blends

Name_____

Read the words below. Then look at the pictures. Write the word that tells about each picture.

drum   sled   desk   flag   snake
crab   nest   plate   frog

 crab	 flag	 snake
 sled	 frog	 desk
 drum	 plate	 nest

98

Vowel Pairs: AI and AY

Name_____

Train has the long-**a** sound spelled **ai**. **Hay** has the long-**a** sound spelled **ay**.

train   hay

Read the words and look at the pictures. Circle the word that tells about each picture.

(rain) ray		train (tray)		mail (nail)	
(sail) say		plain (play)		(mail) may	
(snail) sail		tray (trail)		brain (braid)	
(rail) ray		(tail) trail		claim (clay)	

99

Vowel Pairs: EE and EA

Name_____

Bee has the long-**e** sound spelled **ee**. **Bean** has the long-**e** sound spelled **ea**.

bee   bean

Read the words and look at the pictures. Circle the word that tells about each picture.

see (seat)		(meat) neat		sea (seal)	
(feet) fee		(beak) bee		(sleep) seat	
tea team		bee (beet)		(jeep) jeans	
(peas) peel		heat (heel)		leap (leaf)	

100

151

Review: AI, AY, EE, and EA

Name_____

Read the words and look at the pictures. Circle the word that tells about each picture.

sail / say / (seal) / see		pay / (pail) / peel / peas		(bee) / beat / beak / beef	
tail / team / (tea) / tray		(mail) / may / meat / meet		ray / (rain) / read / real	
(play) / pay / pain / pail		train / tray / rain / (tree)		(hay) / heat / heel / hail	

Vowel Pairs: OA and OW

Name_____

Coat has the long-o sound spelled **oa**.
Window has the long-o sound spelled **ow**.

coat   window

Read the words and look at the pictures. Circle the word that tells about each picture.

boat / (bowl)		snow / (soap)		(goat) / grow	
crow / (coat)		row / road		(float) / flow	
blow / (bow)		tow / (toad)		(crow) / coal	
(load) / low		slow / (snow)		oak / (oats)	

Vowel Pairs: OO

Name_____

The sound you hear in the middle of **moon** is spelled by the letters **oo**.

moon

Name the pictures. Write **oo** below each picture whose name has the **oo** sound as in **moon**.

zoo	goat	tooth
OO		OO
raccoon	boot	spoon
OO	OO	OO
moose	lamp	broom
OO		OO

Vowel Pairs: OO

Name_____

The sound you hear in the middle of **book** is spelled by the letters **oo**.

book

Name the pictures. Write **oo** below each picture whose name has the **oo** sound, as in **book**.

football	hook	tray
OO	OO	
foot	rope	saw
OO		
hood	bed	wood
OO		OO

Vowel Pairs: OO

Name_____

Read the words and name the pictures. Draw a line from each word to the picture it names.

m**oo**n   b**oo**k

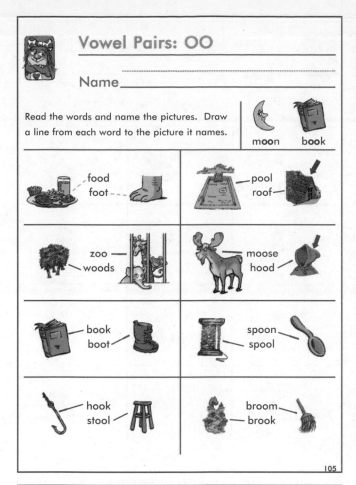

food
foot

pool
roof

zoo
woods

moose
hood

book
boot

spoon
spool

hook
stool

broom
brook

105

Review: OA, OW, and OO

Name_____

Read the words and name the pictures. Circle the word that names each picture.

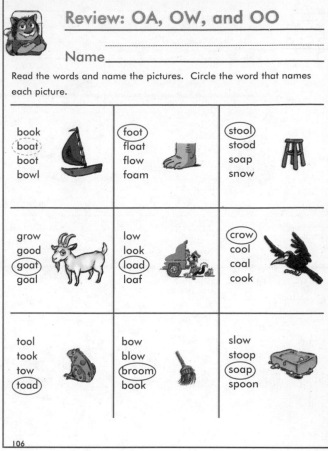

book	foot	stool
boat	float	stood
boot	flow	soap
bowl	foam	snow

grow	low	crow
good	look	cool
goat	load	coal
goal	loaf	cook

tool	bow	slow
took	blow	stoop
tow	broom	soap
toad	book	spoon

106

A Sound of Y

Name_____

The letter **y** at the end of some words can stand for the long-**i** sound, as in **fly**.

fly

Name the pictures. Write **y** below each picture whose name has the long-**i** sound, as in **fly**.

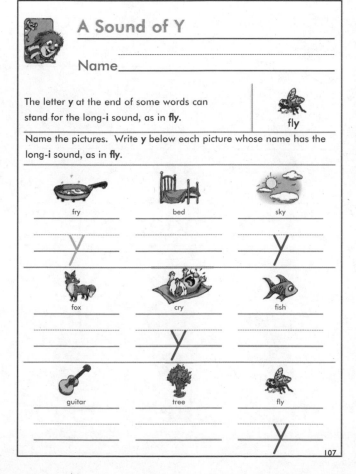

fry

bed

sky

fox

cry

fish

guitar

tree

fly

107

A Sound of Y

Name_____

The letter **y** at the end of some words can stand for the long-**e** sound, as in **pony**.

pony

Name the pictures. Write **y** below each picture whose name has the long-**e** sound, as in **pony**.

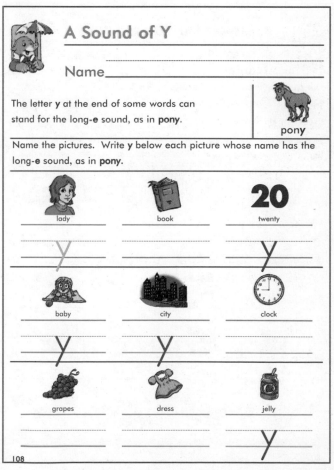

lady

book

20
twenty

baby

city

clock

grapes

dress

jelly

108

153

Two Sounds of Y

Name_____

Read the words and look at the pictures. Circle the word that tells about each picture.

fly   pony

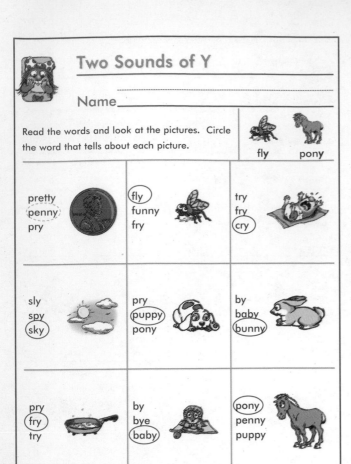

pretty (penny) pry		(fly) funny fry		try (fry) (cry)	
sly spy (sky)		pry (puppy) pony		by baby (bunny)	
pry (fry) try		by bye (baby)		pony penny puppy	

Progress Check: Vowel Pairs and Sounds of Y

Name_____

Read the words and name the picture. Circle the word that names each picture.

(mail) mow		(snail) snow		(try) tray	
see (seal)		bee by		(boat) book	
(soap) seem		bait (boot)		hair (hook)	
(bunny) bean		stay (sky)		(baby) by	

Consonant Pairs: SH and CH

Name_____

The sound at the beginning of **shoe** is spelled by the letters **sh**. The sound at the beginning of **chair** is spelled by the letters **ch**.

shoe   chair

Name the pictures. In each row, circle the picture or pictures that begin with the same sound as the first picture.

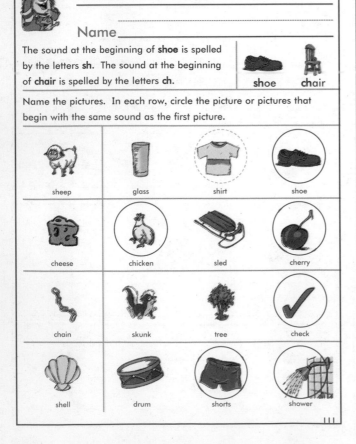

sheep	glass	shirt	shoe
cheese	chicken	sled	cherry
chain	skunk	tree	check
shell	drum	shorts	shower

Consonant Pairs: SH and CH

Name_____

Read the words below and look at the pictures. Write the word that tells about each picture.

ship	shave	chain
sheep	chop	chin
cheek	shell	shed

shoe   chair

chain	sheep	shell
cheek	ship	chop
shave	shed	chin

154

Consonant Pairs: TH and WH

Name_____

The sound at the beginning of **thin** is spelled by the letters **th**. The sound at the beginning of **wheel** is spelled by the letters **wh**.

 thin   wheel

Name the pictures. In each row, circle the picture or pictures that begin with the same sound as the first picture.

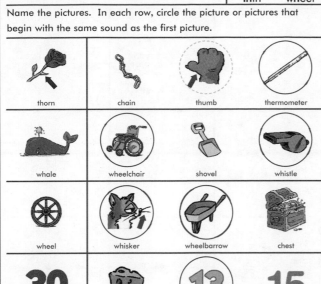

thorn	chain	thumb	thermometer
whale	wheelchair	shovel	whistle
wheel	whisker	wheelbarrow	chest
thirty	cheese	thirteen	fifteen

113

Consonant Pairs: TH and WH

Name_____

Name the pictures. Write the letters that stand for the beginning sound of each picture name.

thin   wheel

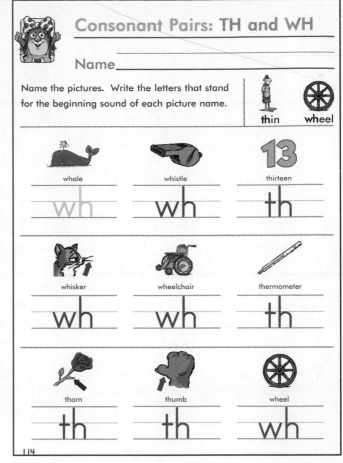

whale	whistle	thirteen
wh	wh	th
whisker	wheelchair	thermometer
wh	wh	th
thorn	thumb	wheel
th	th	wh

114

Consonant Pairs: Final SH, CH, and TH

Name_____

The sound at the end of **wish** is spelled by the letters **sh**.
The sound at the end of **each** is spelled by the letters **ch**.
The sound at the end of **with** is spelled by the letters **th**.

wish
each
with

Name the pictures. In each row, circle the picture or pictures that end with the same sound as the first picture.

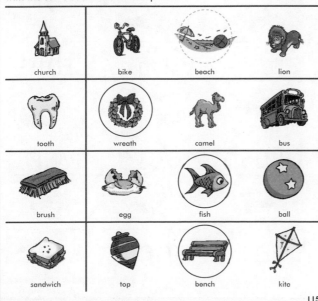

church	bike	beach	lion
tooth	wreath	camel	bus
brush	egg	fish	ball
sandwich	top	bench	kite

115

Consonant Pairs: Final SH, CH, and TH

Name_____

Name the pictures. Write the letters that stand for the ending sound of each picture name.

wish
each
with

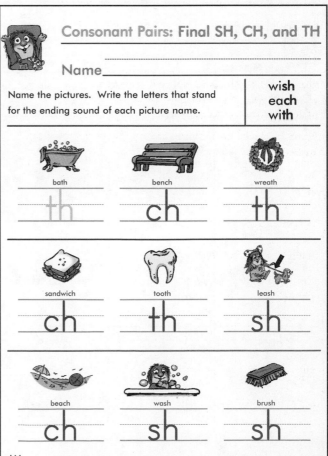

bath	bench	wreath
th	ch	th
sandwich	tooth	leash
ch	th	sh
beach	wash	brush
ch	sh	sh

116

Consonant Pairs: NG

Name_____

The sound at the end of **ring** is spelled by the letters **ng**.

ring

Name the pictures. Circle each picture whose name ends with **ng**.

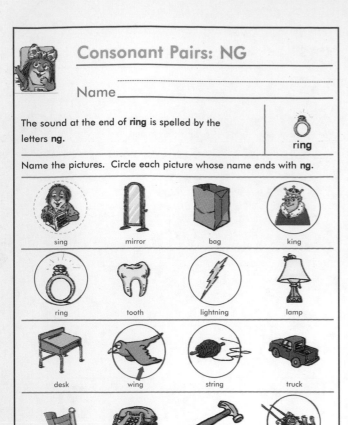

sing	mirror	bag	king
ring	tooth	lightning	lamp
desk	wing	string	truck
flag	telephone	hammer	swing

117

Consonant Pairs: NG

Name_____

Read the words and look at the pictures. Circle the word that tells about each picture.

ring

(swing) sing	(wing) sing	bang (hang)
sting (king)	(sting) swing	(sing) bring
(song) ring	wing (string)	(ring) king

118

Review: SH, CH, TH, WH, and NG

Name_____

Read the words and look at the pictures. Circle the word that tells about each picture.

(wing) sing bring ring	(chain) when then shape	chin (thin) whip ship
math (bath) with path	(fish) dish wash push	(whale) shave cheese these
inch each (bench) beach	(sheep) cheap wheat that	ring wing sing (swing)

119

Progress Check: SH, CH, TH, WH, and NG

Name_____

Read the words below. Then look at the pictures. Write the word that tells about each picture.

ship	chain	thin	swing	shell
bench	wheel	brush	tooth	

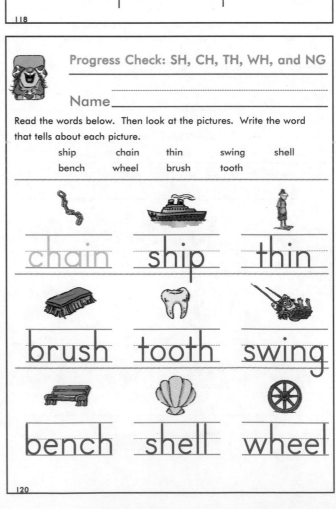

chain	ship	thin
brush	tooth	swing
bench	shell	wheel

120

156

McGraw-Hill Children's Publishing

All our workbooks meet school curriculum guidelines and correspond to The McGraw-Hill Companies classroom textbooks.

SPECTRUM SERIES

DOLCH Sight Word Activities

The DOLCH Sight Word Activities Workbooks use the classic Dolch list of 220 basic vocabulary words that make up from 50% to 75% of all reading matter that children ordinarily encounter. Since these words are ordinarily recognized on sight, they are called *sight words*. Volume 1 includes 110 sight words. Volume 2 covers the remainder of the list. Over 160 pages.

TITLE	ISBN	PRICE
Grades K-1 Vol. 1	1-57768-429-X	$9.95
Grades K-1 Vol. 2	1-57768-439-7	$9.95

GEOGRAPHY

Full-color, three-part lessons strengthen geography knowledge and map reading skills. Focusing on five geographic themes including location, place, human/environmental interaction, movement, and regions. Over 150 pages. Glossary of geographical terms and answer key included.

TITLE	ISBN	PRICE
Gr 3, Communities	1-57768-153-3	$7.95
Gr 4, Regions	1-57768-154-1	$7.95
Gr 5, USA	1-57768-155-X	$7.95
Gr 6, World	1-57768-156-8	$7.95

MATH

Features easy-to-follow instructions that give students a clear path to success. This series has comprehensive coverage of the basic skills, helping children to master math fundamentals. Over 150 pages. Answer key included.

TITLE	ISBN	PRICE
Grade 1	1-57768-111-8	$7.95
Grade 2	1-57768-112-6	$7.95
Grade 3	1-57768-113-4	$7.95
Grade 4	1-57768-114-2	$7.95
Grade 5	1-57768-115-0	$7.95
Grade 6	1-57768-116-9	$7.95
Grade 7	1-57768-117-7	$7.95
Grade 8	1-57768-118-5	$7.95

PHONICS

Provides everything children need to build multiple skills in language. Focusing on phonics, structural analysis, and dictionary skills, this series also offers creative ideas for using phonics and word study skills in other language arts. Over 200 pages. Answer key included.

TITLE	ISBN	PRICE
Grade K	1-57768-120-7	$7.95
Grade 1	1-57768-121-5	$7.95
Grade 2	1-57768-122-3	$7.95
Grade 3	1-57768-123-1	$7.95
Grade 4	1-57768-124-X	$7.95
Grade 5	1-57768-125-8	$7.95
Grade 6	1-57768-126-6	$7.95

Prices subject to change without notice.

READING

This full-color series creates an enjoyable reading environment, even for below-average readers. Each book contains captivating content, colorful characters, and compelling illustrations, so children are eager to find out what happens next. Over 150 pages. Answer key included.

TITLE	ISBN	PRICE
Grade K	1-57768-130-4	$7.95
Grade 1	1-57768-131-2	$7.95
Grade 2	1-57768-132-0	$7.95
Grade 3	1-57768-133-9	$7.95
Grade 4	1-57768-134-7	$7.95
Grade 5	1-57768-135-5	$7.95
Grade 6	1-57768-136-3	$7.95

SPELLING

This full-color series links spelling to reading and writing and increases skills in words and meanings, consonant and vowel spellings, and proofreading practice. Over 200 pages. Speller dictionary and answer key included.

TITLE	ISBN	PRICE
Grade 1	1-57768-161-4	$7.95
Grade 2	1-57768-162-2	$7.95
Grade 3	1-57768-163-0	$7.95
Grade 4	1-57768-164-9	$7.95
Grade 5	1-57768-165-7	$7.95
Grade 6	1-57768-166-5	$7.95

WRITING

Lessons focus on creative and expository writing using clearly stated objectives and pre-writing exercises. Eight essential reading skills are applied. Activities include main idea, sequence, comparison, detail, fact and opinion, cause and effect, and making a point. Over 130 pages. Answer key included.

TITLE	ISBN	PRICE
Grade 1	1-57768-141-X	$7.95
Grade 2	1-57768-142-8	$7.95
Grade 3	1-57768-143-6	$7.95
Grade 4	1-57768-144-4	$7.95
Grade 5	1-57768-145-2	$7.95
Grade 6	1-57768-146-0	$7.95
Grade 7	1-57768-147-9	$7.95
Grade 8	1-57768-148-7	$7.95

TEST PREP
From the Nation's #1 Testing Company

Prepares children to do their best on current editions of the five major standardized tests. Activities reinforce test-taking skills through examples, tips, practice, and timed exercises. Subjects include reading, math, and language. Over 150 pages. Answer key included.

TITLE	ISBN	PRICE
Grade 1	1-57768-101-0	$8.95
Grade 2	1-57768-102-9	$8.95
Grade 3	1-57768-103-7	$8.95
Grade 4	1-57768-104-5	$8.95
Grade 5	1-57768-105-3	$8.95
Grade 6	1-57768-106-1	$8.95
Grade 7	1-57768-107-X	$8.95
Grade 8	1-57768-108-8	$8.95

LANGUAGE ARTS

Encourages creativity and builds confidence by making writing fun! Seventy-two four-part lessons strengthen writing skills by focusing on parts of speech, word usage, sentence structure, punctuation, and proofreading. Each level includes a *Writer's Handbook* at the end of the book that offers writing tips. This series is based on the highly respected SRA/McGraw-Hill language arts series. More than 180 full-color pages.

TITLE	ISBN	PRICE
Grade 2	1-57768-472-9	$7.95
Grade 3	1-57768-473-7	$7.95
Grade 4	1-57768-474-5	$7.95
Grade 5	1-57768-475-3	$7.95
Grade 6	1-57768-476-1	$7.95

Prices subject to change without notice.